AGNOSTICS ANONYMOUS

KENNETH PALMER

Agnostics Anonymous

LONDON
NEVILLE SPEARMAN

First published in Great Britain
by Neville Spearman Ltd
112 Whitfield Street, London, W.1

© 1969 by Kenneth Palmer

Set in 11 pt Baskerville 2 point leaded and
printed by Clarke, Doble & Brendon Ltd, Plymouth.
Bound by G. & J. Kitcat Ltd, London.

CONTENTS

	Page
INTRODUCTION	9
THE FOCUS	23
COMMENTARY	31
The Nature of Revelation	33
The Day of Reckoning : Memory : Destiny	37
The Last Death and Beyond : The Living Darkness	41
Evil and Sin	45
Outlook on Death	51
Children	54
Prayer	59
Lust for Power	61
Indivisibility of God	63
Love	65
No Hell for Animals	67
The Indwelling Entity	70
Sleep	73
Transition Link : From Risen Ape to God	78
The Inward Search	83
A Scientific Approach to God	89
INTERIM	95
CHRISTIANITY IN FOCUS	103
The Bible : Creation and the Fall	105
The Bible : Adam, Eve, The Garden and The Serpent	112
The Bible : Free-choice and Original Sin	121
Reincarnation	123

CONTENTS

	Page
Heaven	130
Compulsion without Conviction	132
The Holy Ghost and the Holy Spirit	134
Virgin Birth	137
A FEW SHORT THOUGHTS AND APHORISMS	139
CONCLUSION	145
MEDITATION	160

If when I die you weep, then you must weep
For those who live, but living, yet are dead :
For in the moment when my breath shall cease
And I have no more body, no more head;
Nor feet shall run astray, nor thoughts confuse,
Nor eyes bewildered be by truth pervert;
Nor ears reflect the lying sounds of earth,
Nor fingers touch the seemingly inert;
In that day shall I find the life I know
But as a partial state, and in that day
Shall take that which is mine, and nevermore
Be parted, for it will be mine for aye :
The last death overcome, the sting removed,
The dust left for another one to slake :
On that day do not weep for me, for I
Have but done what all must do, for God's sake.

INTRODUCTION

Every man in his time must search for Truth. Sometime to everyone it becomes urgent to know who he is, what he is, where he comes from, and where he is going. The meanings of life and death, heaven and hell, God and man, pain and suffering, reason and purpose. He knows when he reaches a certain stage of development, that each individual human being must find and face his God alone. No-one can mediate for him, and no-one share in his final reckoning.

This book is the result of a search by one man, who was unable to accept religion as offered by the Christian Church, because he found it too limited, and because he demanded intellectual, as well as emotional satisfaction, and refused to give complete faith until reason had been to a high degree satisfied. The search was a long one, but he is now satisfied that God loves an honest doubter.

Had it been possible, the book would have been written in a strictly impersonal manner throughout. It is not possible however, as the whole of it hinges on personal experience of an, apparently, unusual nature, or at least with an unusual outcome. The first person singular will, then, obtrude itself occasionally and without further apology. That being so, it were better over and done with as soon as possible, and this introduction therefore will be a short personal background, limited to some events of a psychic or spiritual nature which seem to have had a bearing on subsequent development.

My parents lived a decent life, but did not attend any place of worship. From the age of four years however, I was sent to the nearest religious establishment, a Methodist chapel. Regular attendance through the Sunday School, the Young Men's Class, the Christian Endeavour etc., were followed in turn by the adult developments of teaching in the Sunday School, singing in the choir, playing for the cricket team, publicly praying in Prayer Meetings, and even considering the possibility of lay preaching. Gradually however, over the course of a few years, I found myself less and less able to accept the doctrinal teaching, until eventually, at the age of twenty-one years, rather troubled about it but considering that any other course would be hypocritical, I severed connection.

By this time, that which I could have believed in was so overlaid by all which appeared to me to be artificial, that it appeared hopeless. It just did not have the clear ring of truth. It sounded cracked. The Apostles' creed I could not honestly accept. The Virgin Birth, The Ascension, the final judgment through Christ, The Trinity, The Resurrection of the body, all these were beyond my capacity for superstition, for as such, in part at least, I regarded them. The Fall and its consequences made me really angry. I simply would not feel guilty, and therefore, for me, the conception of the Fall was wrong. Similarly, I could not accept that any sacrifice excepting my own, could atone for such wrong as I might do. I felt too, that if the revelation through Jesus were really unique, final and complete, then it was a poor reflection on the efficacy of God, that he should have left us with such little understanding. For, and this really infuriated me, almost invariably when I asked a reasonable and intelligent question about reason and purpose, the only answers usually forthcoming were that, 'It is not given to us to understand—' or, 'Our finite minds are unable to grasp—', or, 'We must have faith'. How many times I heard this last, I shudder to remember, for I was never given any reasonable grounds for faith.

Through most of these seventeen years (4 to 21 years old), I had been carried along by the play on emotions which had been exercised by this religion. In the end I revolted, and summing up something like what has been written, I decided that if I could not find something better than this, and in particular a better God than portrayed by Christianity, then I would risk eternal damnation rather than live with a belief, which to me, was completely mistaken.

For two extremely busy years I left it behind me, living decently but without allegiance to any religious body, and without attending any place of worship. For over 30 years I never again even looked into a Bible.

10

When I was twenty-three years old my father died. He had been a happy man though in poor circumstances, and so far as I know never willingly hurt anyone and was, on the contrary, always ready to help. He and I got along reasonably well, but quarrelled at times, probably as much as the average father and son. After some months of illness culminating in a few weeks of agony, he died. My mother and I sat up with him on alternate nights for the last few weeks, for when the pains were at their worst he had to be held down until a new dose of drugs took effect. Unlike today, drugs then were administered only when the pain became unbearable. Holding him was beyond my mother's strength, so that if it was necessary during my rest nights she had to wake me from time to time. I was tall and strong, and my father rapidly wasting away, but to hold him during these periods meant digging my heels into the bedroom carpet, and exerting all my strength. We buried him, and for a week I was numb. Then, for the first time, I really faced my God, or rather, the God which Christianity had offered me, the only one which, so far, I knew. I told Him that if this was a sample of what He caused to happen, or even allowed to happen without understood reason, I wanted none of Him. If we are all sinful and must be punished, and if that was His punishment of my father for the, apparently, kindly fifty-one years of earthly life he had led, then He was far from being the loving, the merciful and the just God depicted by Christianity. If, I told Him, a man were to be punished for faults of which he was conscious, that could be just. If, however, he was to be punished for the sins of others before him, and for no seeming faults of his own, that was rank injustice, and I would have none of it. I had been told that Jesus had suffered so that we could be forgiven. Was this a sample of forgiveness? That my father, physically at any rate, and perhaps mentally too from sheer puzzlement and frustration, should suffer possibly as much as had Jesus? Just what good had Jesus done? No-one had been able to give me a good logical reason based on justice, why the individual should be held to be born in sin, and to remain in sin. Until that was done I just refused to have that feeling of guilt which is inherent in Christianity. Either the conception of God given me by Christianity was a wrong conception or, if it were right, I was finished with Him. So we parted.

I became an Agnostic and remained so for thirty years, touching atheism at one period though not for long. As there is confusion of meaning between these two words, let me give my intended definitions. An Atheist denies the existence of God or a First Cause, or at best denies the possibility of knowing Him or It. An Agnostic makes no denial, but refuses to believe further than that for which he can find evidence capable of being apprehended by his mind. For me however it is not sufficient that one should just have the outlook of an Agnostic. That is only sitting on the fence. I had actively to seek for evidence, and did so with an extremely sceptical outlook.

In retrospect it is evident that I began to dig my way through on two separate lines. These were, firstly Spiritualism, and secondly writing verse. To take them separately, when attending a few Spiritualist meetings, I was given one or two 'messages' purporting to be from the spirit world. One of these I found was checkable, although it involved a fairly considerably amount of work and time. It was of such a nature that made it almost impossible that the medium could have known about it previously, and I decided that, if I could prove it to be correct, then I would consider Spiritualism worth further investigation. In short it was so proved, and I went on a little further although not much, for I left the country for some years and on return have never attended such a meeting again. In all I attended no more than about six meetings. I have never witnessed table-rapping, never seen apparitions, never felt anything physically, and never felt anything touch me. However, the germ having been laid, perhaps made me receptive some nine or so years later, to the persuasion of a friend to attempt to use a planchette. She was able to, although she did not own one at the time. This, by the way, was when I was about thirty-three years of age. I made a planchette, bought a roll of white wall paper (lining paper), opened the leaves of a dining table and pinned the paper on, thus giving a five-foot writing width. Extremely sceptically I started, half-chiding myself for being such a fool, and half-grinning at the apparent farce of it. Never has a grin been wiped off anyone's face more quickly for, in response to my first question, the thing moved, gained speed, made a complete line of scribble and ran off the table edge. Picked up and placed at the beginning again under the first line, and asked to, 'Please continue', it did so and wrote several lines. When finished it stopped dead, and nothing I could do would start it again. We (self, wife and friend), then turned our attention to the scribble, and I found that it really was one continuous line of letters of the alphabet in a handwriting quite dissimilar from mine. We then divided this up with a pencil, for sure enough it divided into words, the words made sense, and the whole was answers to questions I had asked of it. The first occasion was a shock, but the use of it became commonplace. Certain rules had to be followed, rules found by experience such as, it was useless asking for any information which would result in personal financial gain. For instance when asked the result of a horse race, etc., the planchette would remain completely dead. In passing I may say that, being so sceptical, I had from the start been extremely careful not in any way to assist the movement of the planchette, resting the tips of my fingers on it so lightly that they barely touched it. Not only that, but I did not think about the questions after asking them, and also asked mainly those to which I did not know the answers. What made me doubly sure that I was not actuating the thing, was the speed at which it operated. I am a fast writer, but if it had been possible for me to have sat with a fountain pen and competed with it, I am sure it would have beaten me. It almost, in fact, ran away with me and I had not the faintest idea, until all was over and the writing divided up and copied out, what had been written.

So far so good. I was satisfied that something other than my conscious self actuated this thing. But what of the answers received? Many of them could not be checked. Checking some meant waiting sometimes for longish periods. Some, it was possible to check more or less at once. I did all I could in this respect and can only say that of results checked, a small proportion only, I did not find one wrong. I was able to receive through or from, in all; four 'guides' as I believe they are called. At first it was one, and I asked for and received his name and various details about him. Then, one day, the answers came in a totally different hand-writing. This was somewhat startling and I asked who was writing now. The name etc., was given as for the first one. From then on I never knew who would answer a question. Sometimes one, sometimes the other, but my request for one or the other would usually be sufficient to bring him in (both names were of men). Much later on another handwriting started up, but this time with painful slowness and with ill-formed rather shaky letters. This, I was told on enquiry, was my father. So it went on, one or other coming in at my request, and although my wife and I checked constantly and carefully, we were never able to fault the three handwritings. Each was quite different from the others in form, angle, etc. Each had its own idiosyncrasies and they never varied. Considering the speed at which the writing came, this was sufficient confirmation for me that I did not consciously cause the movements. Of that much I was now quite certain.

As an experiment I next tried the same technique of questions and answers but without the planchette. In its place I held a soft-leaded pencil loosely in my hand, then asked a question and waited. It worked, but slowly, and I did not develop this very far. Next I cut out the verbal questions and merely thought them. The answers came as before. Then without any equipment at all I sat quite still, thought a question and received in thought, an answer. This I started to develop, because it fitted in with the parallel line of verse writing, of which more later.

With the development of the thought process the whole thing suddenly collapsed. Whether because of the thought process, or whether because of something else which happened about that time, I shall never know for sure. The friend mentioned before had a 'guide'. I forget the name, but it was female and it appeared to be of tremendous verve and energy, for the handwriting, which was rounded and quite distinctly feminine in character, fairly bounced across the paper at a speed exceeding any of mine. Being intrigued and amused by this I began sometimes to ask her to answer my questions. The request was complied with several times and then, quite suddenly, all died. Every little bit went dead. The planchette became once more the inanimate thing it had been when I first made it, and it never moved again. It was a great shock, and I decided that it was of my own making in that I had not been satisfied with my own 'guides', but had asked for that of my friend. Looking back, I don't believe that it was so, though no doubt it was a good lesson nevertheless. It ended I believe because, firstly, out of it had developed a technique which was to be necessary for further progress and, secondly, because though I did not know it at the time, these things such as Spiritualism, Faith-healing and Magic are all cul-de-sacs off the straight road through to the truly intuitive. Become too involved or engrossed in one of them, then, unable to or not wishing to, turn round and go back, you will never find the straight road on again. If I had persisted longer with Spiritualism, would the response have returned again? I shall never know, and am content. Many years after this, in fact after I had found the truly intuitive way, I was sorely tempted to investigate another cul-de-sac, that of Faith-healing, for by that time my wife had become crippled with arthritis. I did make a tentative attempt but did not presevere because I felt, no, I knew, that it would check me on the main path. I told my wife I would not go on trying, and she, God bless her, acquiesced.

Now to finish off the planchette phase. The instrument was put away and forgotten. Nearly twenty years later, after removals through several different houses and districts, I suddenly thought of the thing again. This was also after I had found the intuitive way. I suddenly remembered it and asked my wife if we still had it. She didn't know, but thought it had been thrown away. Not satisfied, I tried the thought question, thought answer, technique, and received a reply immediately to look in the third drawer from the bottom in a chest of drawers in a certain bedroom. This I passed on to my wife and went out to work. When I came home the planchette was on the table. I rigged up a sheet of paper, placed the planchette on it, finger-tips on the surface lightly, and asked a question. I've forgotten the question. All I remember is a sudden excruciating pain like a knife-wound in the region of the left kidney. Never before or since have I experienced such a pain. The planchette died, that is, was burned, that night.

Returning to the point where the instrumental phase, if it may be so called, ended, and the thought to thought phase started. This I developed very slowly over the years, not too seriously, occasionally finding something which was lost by the thought query and answer method, but only really playing with it, until gradually I found that sometimes when I thought a question, a spot of white light accompanied the answer. In those days I closed my eyes, no doubt to assist concentration. Then occasionally I became aware of the spot of light, sometimes in bed at night when I had not asked a question. It occurred to me, therefore, that perhaps this was a sign of desired communication from the other end. So whenever I saw the light I began to ask whoever was concerned to give me a message and, sure enough, messages started to come through, and there commenced slowly, a two-way system capable of being initiated from either end. Can those of you who have never experienced anything like this imagine what it means? The implications of it, when realized, stop a man dead in his tracks. It's terrific! It continued over a number of years, never known by anyone excepting myself and my wife, and as it developed, I was told that it was my father, and the light was his sign.

Before leaving this record of the reciprocal method of communication, I must add something of a like nature which occurred countless times later over the fourteen or fifteen months of the revelation. At the start of this intuitive reception I used to close my eyes, finding it easier to concentrate thus. As it became easier, I kept the eyes open and have done so ever since. After closing the eyes, I would then stop all thought. Then, not of my volition, the cheeks would suddenly rise, nipping the eyes tightly shut for a few seconds, before relaxing again. Then communication would commence, usually for a short period in those early elementary days, by way of question and answer, with all thought rather laboriously held in check. This soon developed into a flow, with the change over made without conscious effort. However, this nipping of the eyes became an invariable prelude to a period of

16

communication, and if I did not receive this, I had to postpone the session and try again some time later. Then after a while the same thing happened as had happened with the light. Sometimes, right out of the blue, unsought, would come a nipping of the eyes, not because of anything initiated by me, not of my volition, and I would immediately or as soon as possible prepare, and sure enough, always, there was a communication. Thus again it became a reciprocal arrangement. The need for any such signs soon ceased, as intuitional reception became more constant and thought was reduced accordingly.

Returning now to the days of the light.

When it first began I used to tell my wife about it, though not in full detail. Later on, whenever I had a message or the answer to a query, I would pass it on to her immediately, so that she could act as an independent check on the correctness of the answers. Do not think this was an everyday occurrence for it was not. It happened only occasionally, for I never asked advice on anything which was not important. The previous question and answer business of asking where lost things might be found etc., was separate from this and was still used intermittently, but only very occasionally. My wife is the only one who can bear witness to it and then not in detail for we kept no written records, but over a period of a number of years, I received really important advice and guidance through this channel. Then I found the way through, and the need for this ceased and has never been, and will never be used again.

That then, briefly, is the one line along which I worked.

The second line, that of writing verse, started somewhere in my late 'teens. At first very occasional short verses gradually increasing in length and in quality, though never perhaps of much worth to anyone but myself. To me, as I can see now, looking back, they were invaluable. Firstly they gave a productive line of thought to work on. Where did the verse come from and how did it come and why? For the serious verse I wrote was not mechanically constructed. I have written loads of trashy mechanical jingles and humorous verses etc., but they were, and still are, in an entirely different category. The serious verse came from

17

I knew not where, but it was not consciously mine. What I needed to do was, when the environment was suitable, to make myself receptive. First, however, I had to have ready sharpened pencils and plenty of paper. Then I sat and waited, 'making my mind a blank', as I always put it in those days. Then, if I were lucky, something would come through. All I needed to do was to write it down, trying hard to keep pace with it, for at times it used to race and I had perforce to omit words in order to keep up, going back over it afterwards and filling in as best I could. At other times it would start on its own, so that I found it necessary at all times to carry pencil and paper around with me. Remarkably too, many a score of times whilst I have been doing routine work such as inspecting objects and memorizing figures to be tabulated later, verse has come rushing through my mind so that, when I paused to tabulate the results of my work, as soon as I had done that I had then to take pencil and paper and write down twenty or thirty lines of verse, which had accumulated in the fifteen or so minutes previously. I became accustomed to this 'double-working', but have never found an explanation for it. Whatever came had to be written down immediately, or it was lost without a trace. It was almost like sudden intermittent unveilings of portions of a film. Over the years I accumulated a great store of these verses, and also some prose including some short stories, mainly humorous. After what I call my enlightenment and the commencement of consciously controlled intuitive working, I decided that the best thing to do with all the material thus accumulated was to burn it, which I did sometime in 1960 I think. Most of it was written in thick, foolscap sized notebooks, several of which were burned, together with masses of loose copy. Sometime later I came across a few sheets in the loft which had been overlooked. Re-reading them, it occurred to me that they might be worth keeping, solely as an indication of the way my mind was working at a particular period, for I had always dated all material. A few therefore still exist with dates 1933, 1934, 1935, 1941 etc. During the period of the revelation, that is 1960 and part of 1961, a number of poems came through, of which four short ones are included in this book. The remainder are omitted as being, possibly, out of place here.

In addition to giving me a fruitful line of thought, this verse writing with the accompanying condition of 'blankness of mind' gave me, over the years, much practice in this mind preparation, and this was eventually to prove invaluable as, when suddenly I knew how it should be used, I shot ahead at great speed. At that time however, happy though I was to have these periods of receptivity, I found it very frustrating that I was able to 'receive' only occasionally, and not as and when I wished to do so. The result was that sometimes for long periods I would dismiss it all, and refuse to have anything to do with it.

So then, this way and the way through Spiritualism continued slowly and spasmodically for thirty years. All the time I was trying to think through it all, and to formulate some ideas of the why and the wherefore. Then one night just about on my fifty-third birthday, a friend who knew little or nothing of all this, came to me one night with a book which he had been reading, and asked for my opinion on it. Not particularly interested I started to read, but had read only part way through the book when I suddenly dropped it for, in a flash, I knew what had been happening to me most of my life. I had been coming into contact intermittently with the source of intuitive knowledge which is in us all. The results I had been having were extremely distorted because the instrument receiving them, myself, was extremely distorted despite the way in which I tried to prepare. Now, if I was right and I could start to prepare myself properly, I should be able to get through to this intuitive source at will. The book was forgotten and it was, in fact, about two years before I finished reading it. It was not important. Just a few words in it, and I've never found out which they were, proved to be the penny which dropped for me. I set to work at once on preparing myself as I now believed it should be done, and as I thought, I was able from then on to contact, for short periods at a time, but consciously and at will, the source of all intuitive knowledge— the immense storehouse of Truth, of all from before time began. Slowly and dimly it came through at first, and I could hold the receptivity for only comparatively short periods, but gradually they lengthened, reception became clearer, and I started to record the results. After a while the technique of making myself receptive became so much a matter of routine, that I was able to switch on and off as quickly as an electric lamp is switched on and off. This went on for between fourteen and fifteen months, and I recorded in writing approximately 300,000 words of raw material of which the majority was a personal revelation. Here I must say that, at first, I did not realize that most of it was purely personal, nor did I know its purpose, nor where it came from. It seemed to come from outside, or as the direct word of God. It needed one or two friendly hints from someone I've met only once so far, to set me quickly on the right track. And how very slight they were! I'm sure deliberately and wisely. There was much more of it than is written in this book, for the personal part was a purging process which cleared out of me previous misconceptions, prejudices and warped outlooks, and left me able to interpret with greater clarity and surety. More of this will be gathered as the book is read. When the several hundreds of apparently disconnected passages recorded were read as a whole, it became apparent that a thread ran through them, obvious in some parts, almost hidden in others, which, when picked out and enlarged upon, revealed a story which was not just personal, but which was surely, I decided, intended for mankind generally. The disentangling and expansion of the thread was a long task, and the story needed to be lived with for several years, and submitted as a whole, and also piece by piece, to the tests of reason before being offered to others. It is not now complete nor, by the very nature of it, can it ever be, but for this one man it is Truth. In it I have found a great peace and a relief from the tension and turmoil, the mental suffering and the frustration, which make up so much of life today. I have found in it a satisfactory philosophy of life, and above all I have found a God which in It's immanence is closer than hands and feet, and which in It's transcendence is just, and although omniscient and indescribable, is yet understandable. So although I have not yet finished, I have reached a stage when I can pause in my search for something better, and during the pause write this book, for I am persuaded that there may be others, not only middle-aged like myself, but also in their 'teens and early twenties, who cannot find intellectual satisfaction in present day religion, and because of that cannot find faith. The days when a religion based on faith alone was sufficient are almost past. Religion has not kept pace with intellectual development and must suffer in the future. Reason it was which made man apart from the animals, and reason it is which must be satisfied today, before the last submission of intellect to intuition can be made.

Of those who now read on I ask only this. Firstly, whatever your present ideas may be, for the time it takes to read this book forget them, and approach the matter with a completely open mind. Secondly, having read it, do not make any immediate decision of any kind. Live with it for at least twelve months, preferably more, before attempting to make an evaluation. Live with it and assimilate slowly. And may you find as great a peace as I have found.

An inconsistency will be found, in that sometimes It, and sometimes He, is used for God. Without doubt of course It is correct, but as, in the past, It has been known to very many for a long time as He, deliberately He has been used sometimes, for it is not objectionably inapplicable, when we see ourselves as units of that force or, symbolically, children of that father.

Whenever the word man is used it should be taken, unless indicated otherwise, as a term for a member of mankind, either male or female.

The Focus

The Focus

There is The Transcendent, The Absolute, and there is, of the Absolute, The Intelligence, that which is called God. And in the Absolute was, in the beginning, all knowledge hidden and all power on leash.

Of this latency, from this Absolute Ground of Being, God created the universe, and Himself entered His creation in a process of It revealing Itself to Itself.

First He created the Mind Image, the Transition Link by means of which, through which, He should eventually return to the original and ever same. And on this Earth the Image was of Man. There was planned a road out to the Image, a physical evolution, the Natural Phase to the summit of the way out, and then on beyond. But the summit of the phase was in Man, the Transition Link, and he was given a separate existence during which he would continue the self-revelation of the Creator, by himself becoming, in measure, a creator. In other words he was to add an extension to the original creation. This would be the Psychic Phase through which he would be independent and self-guided, within limits, before taking the way back by the Spiritual Phase. Thus, so that It, revealing Itself to Itself, might open up further of the inherent latency, the Psychic Phase must be made attractive, so that man would first follow this way, although subject to increasing indicative penalties as he went, for eventually he must return. And the way back must be taken of free-choice, and without the compulsion of strict regulation. So did God blindfold Himself, entering as spiritual entity every part and particle of creation, unconscious of Himself as Himself because of the interposed physical body, with its restricted and limited physical senses between Himself and Truth. And progress through the Natural Phase was planned and regulated, but always within limits allowing a small tolerance, to the stage at which thought and reason developed in the creature called Man, the object of the Image. For this was the Transition Link by means of which

25

God must leave the immutable surge of the Natural Phase, and after a while find, of free-choice and free-will, the way back. And again were laid down laws and regulations, always within limits which, when followed, led back to the original unchanged state. But so that there should be freedom of choice, and also to allow for the creative efforts in man, the Psychic Phase had to be interposed, which would allow man to leave the Natural Phase, and yet reject the promptings of the Spiritual Phase which now began to become apparent. For just as the way out had been compulsorily regulated by instinct, through an inherent knowledge of the way to The Image, so now intuitional guidance became apparent as instinct faded. Now too came suffering as a penalty for exceeding permissible limits, progressively increasing as the limits were further overstepped. And here came freedom of choice, for the powers of the Psychic Phase which allowed man to break free from the Natural Phase, also permitted him to remain free from the regulations of the Spiritual Phase for as long as he chose, thus developing not only an individual entity, but an entity separate in experience from all other individual entities of its kind. And the experience of no two individuals was alike. This developed personality and constant friction between personalities.

In this psychic stage man wanders bemused, enchained by the physical outlook and by sensuous satisfactions, and without constant true guidance, attempting to exercise the terrific latent power which he feels in him. In so doing he sets loose all the savagery of the Natural Phase without the restraint which instinct places upon it, and becomes often lower than the animals. And yet he becomes higher than the animals too for, despite his enslavement to sensuality and the believed freedom of physical existence, he feels also at times the pull of intuitional guidance, and acts upon it.

Here is the only really basic problem of man. He must stay as he is, or he must take the intuitional way back to the original, for he cannot re-enter the Natural Phase. It is folly for a man to think that he is only here for a short seventy or eighty years, for unless and until he wishes otherwise, he is here in this earthly physical and mental hell of frustration for as long as time shall

26

last. For this is Hell, the place of suffering, the place of departed spirits. The only hell a man will ever know, for there is neither pain nor sorrow nor suffering in the purely spiritual state. Here a word of explanation is necessary. That intermission which Christians call Heaven is not a purely spiritual state nor is it a final state. It is still a part of Hell, the difference being in degree. The whole of creation constitutes Hell, Heaven being part of it in intermittent periods free from the physical body and senses and time/space relationships which dominate the time spent in a physical body. Hence Heaven is a relief period during which the spiritual entity can cope with the psychic situation and make retrospective adjustment, or self-judgment, temporarily unfettered by the material. For, in this belief, the soul is not the purely spiritual entity, but is that entity conditioned by the psychic or thought body which, together with the body of flesh in the intermittent periods, insulates it from the return to the original. Thus is permitted its continuous development through many physical lives. For a man is born of the water of the womb not once but many times, sometimes male, sometimes female, until eventually of his own free choice, he is born of the spirit alone and thus can leave his hell for ever. The task is difficult and painful, and may take a long time to accomplish but, on the other hand, by one in an advanced state of development, it may be achieved in his present lifetime. The loss of individuality and personality is the greatest difficulty to be overcome, for that which in pride has been laboriously built up, cannot be cast down suddenly. Very many earthly existences have gone during the shaping of this personality, and man feels that it is precious. For, when at the stage of psychic development at which reason allowed him to break with instinct, he became in truth a living soul. During the Natural Phase the spiritual entity in the individual living creature passes, at the death of the physical body, back to the original, and there is no continuity of development of the individual spiritual entity. The Natural Phase develops or evolves all that which is physical in creation, until the Psychic Phase takes over. There is a long overlap but, from the point at which he takes over, man's evolution ceases to be controlled solely by the regulations of the

Natural Phase, for man is now able to interfere in these, within limits. At the change over the spiritual entity which is not now in animal, but is for the first time in Man, becomes semi-permanently separated from the original ground of being, and now not only for a single life-time. Thus starts the continuous development of an independent spiritual entity. For now man creates a thought body, which insulates the spiritual entity which he is, from the original, and man becomes a separate living soul, so to continue until he himself breaks down, not only the hold of the physical senses, but also this thought barrier or body which he has created, in order to return to the original state. The word body here should not be supposed to mean anything like the physical body, or, indeed, anything at all visible to the human eye. Perhaps aura might be a nearer description than body. Now therefore man, this separate spiritual entity or soul, passes on through fleshy body after fleshy body, not knowing what he is, for each physical re-birth usually wipes out the details of his previous existence. He identifies himself therefore solely with the body which he inhabits, and he believes to be real and basic only that which presents itself through the bodily senses. At each death of a physical body which it inhabits, the soul leaves the body and enters a stage of rest and re-orientation, before being re-born in another physical body for a further life in the flesh. So it goes on, gaining experience, and must so go on until, through the gradually increasing pain, suffering, bewilderment and frustration of this independent, separate, and basically false, existence, it realizes the truth. Then, weary, it turns to the intuitional guidance which will lead it back to the wholly spiritual state from which it sprang, free from the physical aspect at last. This cannot be done until the Ego is surrendered, and the personality so pridefully and painfully built up is crushed. This does not mean oblivion, for in the re-absorbtion into The Aboslute or Transcendent, the little I of the individual becomes the big I of The One Without a Second, and the consciousness of each returning entity becomes the consciousness of The One with which it merges. So there is no loss of consciousness, only a loss of personality. In The One is the store of all knowledge and all wisdom, for as each entity returns, its experience is added to the sum total, which total becomes immediately a part of the entity, as it becomes The One.

Throughout the period of its existence as man, the individual entity helps to create its own intermediate destinies. Its final destiny is to return to the original. It has, however, an intermediate destiny at the end of each earthly cycle, a cycle being a term in the physical body plus a retrospective term out of the physical body, in all the total period from one physical birth to the next. This pre-determined short-term fate for a particular existence in the flesh, is made up of *(a)* general (as opposed to particular), environmental factors, *(b)* hereditary factors and *(c)* consequences of wrong thought or action incurred during the previous existence. The individual, as such, has not usually any control over the first of these. He has some control over the second, but these are governed rather by mankind than by man. The consequences of individual wrong thought and action he must take wholly upon himself, plus a part of group consequences. Consequences depend upon the motivation more than upon the action, therefore those for a particular action will vary with the circumstances. Done in ignorance, a deviation from right may incur only slight consequences, or none, but the same action done with fore-knowledge of its effect, will incur a much more severe penalty. There is justice in all when the viewpoint is big enough to encompass all. The sins of a father visited upon the children, simply means that the consequences of a man's sin in this exis-tence, are mainly carried forward to at least his next incarnation in the flesh through the alignment of intermediate destiny. And let no man say that he acted in ignorance because he did not know what was right or wrong. Intuition, represented here by conscience, will give a right answer to every man who will allow it to rise above thought. This sense which operates in everyone, is pushed under and trodden down because it is inconvenient, and often works at the apparent expense of the individual concerned. It does not really, for if intuition is ignored the long term conse-quences acting upon his future, either in this life on earth or the next, are much greater than the obvious immediate material gain now. There is an absolute standard of conduct which can be attained at any particular time only by a few, while the normal standard varies in the individual according to his stage of development. Action will vary therefore with the individual, as will the consequences. Having attained a working degree of intuitional guidance, it is important that this voice of conscience should be acted upon regardless of the consequences. Have no thought for the morrow. Do what you know it is right for you to do today, and the consequences of your action are out of your hands. The responsibility ceases to be yours. The individual will find himself a happier man. It is, admittedly, difficult to take action which may be damaging to your own immediate welfare, but it pays off in the long run. There are not many with the courage or the conviction to act thus. Only those who have arrived at the stage of development when their experience is sufficient to give them the conviction of this truth, will find it urgent enough to act upon. Yet every man must act upon it sometime. Most have not yet suffered enough, but hell, physical and mental hell, gets hotter every day, and before long, if he does not already, man will need such guidance as this. And for many it will take a long, long time to get out of hell. The more, materially, a man has, the harder it will be, for he has more, materially, to lose by each decision and each action. The more learned a man is the harder it will be, for it will be acknowledging something greater than the intellect and, at the same time, something very simple.

When, by right thought and living, the consequences of previous wrong living have been worked off and a balance struck, it becomes possible for a man to identify himself completely with that which he is. Then, at the next physical death, he passes from the physical/psychical cycle and becomes that, in full knowledge, which he ever was and will be.

Commentary

Commentary

The Nature of Revelation

Revelation is seen from a different angle when it is realized that it is personal and not something sent by a divine external source. It comes of an internal operation. If a man can and will comply with certain rules of moral, ethical and intellectual conduct, he can produce in himself a condition which will result in a personal revelation. This is, as said elsewhere, a huge clearing out operation, a removal of all pre-conceived ideas and all prejudices, which results in a mind so purged and cleansed, that it is enabled to grasp the thin gold thread of intuitive knowledge and guidance which exists all the time, but is hidden from view, the intuitive knowledge of all that is and has been since time everlasting.

Revelation comes of the reaching out of man to God. It is not the bending of God to man. Confusion may arise because the conditions necessary are stillness, such stillness as never normally known, and apparent passivity. What is not generally realized is that in the stillness and passivity, is a degree of alertness and concentration unknown in everyday life.

The long and difficult road back to the original state, has the guide rope of intuition along its whole length. It has been there since before physical creation anl evolution commenced, for it was a part of the original plan to the Mind Image. The way out is mainly by instinct, the way back mainly by intuition. The two are bridged by the intellect.

Those who depend upon faith through revelation for salvation or release, may object, and wish to deny the bridge of the intellect. Nevertheless it is true, for although many may reach salvation through faith, it is at least up to the final point, faith in the intellectual achievement of another, that is, of the one who received the revelation, for revelation usually comes only after long and exhaustive intellectual concentration and effort, to the stage of desperation, ending in surrender to the intuitive after intellectual failure. This surrender to and acceptance of the intuitive, is in itself an act of faith, in this case direct and without an intermediary. The faith required for this last jump is not so great as might be thought, for along the road of preparation will have been many minor proofs of intuitive guidance, each sufficient only to lead on through the intellectual path. The road therefore is long and difficult, but there is no short cut. Moreover, before the final stage is reached, the one seeking it has to pass his final judgment day or day of reckoning while in the flesh, and his slate must be wiped clean or, in other words, his scale must be finally balanced. This is a bitter experience but leaves a man clean for the first time. Simultaneously with the intellectual probing there will have been developing in him, perhaps almost if not entirely unconsciously, the wish to do good works—not spectacular or big works and probably not known to many. He will eschew dishonesty of all description, become less superficial and live a simpler life. He will control bad temper or habits which distress others, give active assistance to those in need of it and in general, will consider his neighbour and become more self-less. All this can come of deliberate effort, or for no obvious reason, and can be quite unconsciously adopted. It is, however, together with the intellectual probing, an essential pre-requisite of acceptance to the higher state of consciousness necessary for enlightenment. Why is all this necessary? Probably partly because one must be essentially honest in all respects, otherwise the truth would be distorted, and partly because one must know mankind through and through in order to understand it. The approach is initated by man and finalized by one who has become temporarily the Son of God, or Immanent God, for it is only after purging that an approach thus near can be made.

So the approach is made by a man who has reached a stage of development which is very nearly ripe, that is who, through gradual intellectual probing and equally gradual intuitional acceptance, has almost reached the point of full identification of himself, or in other words, who has almost broken through the physical-sensual misrepresentation of basic truth. He will have gradually strengthened the conviction that mankind is in a parlous state, and the matter becomes so urgent to him that he intensifies his effort, sometimes at the expense of his health, in an attempt to find enlightenment and guidance. There should be no mistake about it, the guidance does not bend itself to man. He has to reach for it. It is mankind's way of aligning itself with Reality. Just as the individual after each bodily death, aligns itself by a retrospective look at the memory film of its last existence while in close contact with intuitive guidance, so mankind is able to align itself, by a retrospective look at its past, by a member who passes through the normal routine of death, (except that in this case the flesh does not die), and then returns with the information in the form known as revelation. As has been said, the revelation is given by the Immanent God (or Son of God) in the individual. The process can perhaps be compared with archaeology. Excavation with considerable difficulty in the recesses of a dark cavern, will sometimes reveal enough bones to form a recognizable skeleton, which may then be assimilated into the knowledge of the present. The whole process is more scientific than perhaps is generally realized.

Thus it is that revelation is a part of the intuitive return road, is continuous (or at least semi-continuously received) and progressive. It is and must be progressive while one man remains upon the earth. No revelation can be final until mankind completes its task, nor is it unique. There has been a line of revelations through the ages and it will continue.

Great care is necessary in presentation. Revelation as originally received is mainly personal, and much of it is a purging, cleansing process of the mind of the individual. It varies therefore with the traditional pre-conceived beliefs and the environment of the recipient, it must always be coloured by, and, unless great care is taken, can be badly distorted by them. Much is there also of fantasy and all this has to be weeded out. There can be quite a lot in the old time prophetic style, with sonorous phrases and a real air of authority. The style in which this comes, the force of it, and the way in which the words form literally of themselves in the mind, in a loud and declamatory way, so that one would not be surprised if they were accompanied at times by thunder and lightning, make it appear to be coming in from outside. There is no wonder therefore that it has been so often taken as

35

being the literal words of a transcendent God. Most of this type however, is in fact a gigantic mind clearing or cleansing, which breaks down all the deepest prejudices and clears out the clutter. It is the Immanent in man with its new found view, thrashing out all the old distorted stuff, the collection of a lifetime. Once the purpose of this is realized it can be, and what has been written should be, destroyed, even though with some regret, for it applies only to the recipient, and if read by others could be misleading, if they tried to apply it to themselves. The original revelation therefore must, when complete, be interpreted for mankind generally, by the individual receiving it. No-one but he can do this correctly, for no-one but he has access to his experience and knows the circumstances. If the revelation is extensive he must live with it for a number of years, gradually aligning the thread of pure gold in the general revelation from the comparative dross of the personal. The situation can be difficult if health or other reasons make an early death likely. Then it will be a matter for individual judgment. Perhaps a part might be released and the remainder concealed, or the whole prematurely given out before mature re-interpretation by the recipient. This however can cause much frustration and suffering to believers, and can result in distortion of the truth.

The Day of Reckoning:
Memory: Destiny

When a man identifies himself completely with the divine entity which he is, he sees himself for the first time as he is. For the first time he is able to bypass the physical senses, to break through the thought barrier and the sensuous shield which have imprisoned him so long, and to see himself in true perspective in relation to God and to the remainder of mankind. This is indeed a bitter experience. No-one else knows all that he is and has been. Only he knows all that he has thought and done during this present lifetime on earth, how many unsavoury and unwanted memories have been repressed and forgotten for so many years. Much inconsequential detail is retained and used unconsciously in which to bury the unwanted. No event that ever happened to him is completely lost. His individual memory is a body of thoughts representing each and every event of his life, which is with him always and from which, normally, he cannot escape. He can delve into some of it consciously, but not into all while in the flesh. Some has been thrust too deep for normal conscious re-call. It is an individual record, or if you will, writings in the book of life, which accompanies him, and can only be got rid of in one way.

At each earthly death,* events in the material world cease for a man, for he leaves the body with its brain and sensory system, which has been his only means of perceiving material things. He then rests, held and insulated by the thought body, with its record of his past life. With intuitive guidance from the spirit still available, and with the world of flesh and matter temporarily shut out, he is able to absorb the lessons of his past life, and to re-orientate himself. This takes place gradually. Time and space mean nothing to him, for the life he leads temporarily (and it is still life although not in a human body), is not subject to them, for they are the

* See 'Reincarnation' on page 123.

37

accompaniments of physical creation. The soul is therefore now experiencing eternal life, that is, life out of time, and hundreds of years may pass very quickly. All the lessons based on the experience of the previous bodily life are absorbed, and the necessary trend for future progress decided. Until evil is cancelled out there will be the need for further re-birth in the flesh. He is re-born therefore, impressed with a handicap according to the balance struck, and in combination with the heredity of the fleshy line into which he is born. So his life will be comparatively easy or difficult, fraught with suffering and sorrow or comparatively free from them, to the extent called for in the intermediate judgment he made in the resting period. Thus does a man create his own intermediate destinies, and thus are the sins of the father visited upon the children. As mentioned previously in 'The Focus', some other tendencies also affect the alignment of life. With some possible exceptions, the past surface memory record, its lessons having been assimilated and its usefulness therefore over, is obliterated at re-birth.

When, after hundreds or maybe thousands of lives in human form, the time comes when the consequences of evil have been completely balanced, even though this has been in part unconsciously, the day of the last reckoning or judgment, comes. For once this does not occur during a resting period, but during a life in the flesh. The physical life and the fleshy body were provided to serve the purpose of a transition link, and it is while in the flesh that a man must finally identify himself, and consciously align himself for the last time, before he returns freely and finally to the spirit, at last unhampered by an adverse record, and therefore uninsulated. That last judgment day therefore, comes during a man's earthly life, following upon his identification. On that day the memory record of the salient events of the present life is seen by him almost as in a film, and on this last record is a man's judgment completed. Judgment with re-alignment, has been made countless times before but always while out of a physical body and the trend has always, must always have been, progressive. This last judgment therefore, is only on the balance of error as represented by the present life. On this record he judges himself for, before he arrives at this last judgment day he is, he must be, in an advanced state of consciousness, on a spiritual level which allows of impersonal judgment. The bitterness of repentance is dependent on the record which he sees on that day, and on that day he becomes competent in the flesh to judge himself, and on that day is the judgment of God his own judgment. On that day, as God, he sits in judgment on himself. He suffers his self-inflicted remorse, and when the fire and the torment are quenched, he is clean while in the flesh for the first time. As he placed himself in error, so he redeems himself from it. On that day he comes to the beginning of his heritage of spiritual one-ness with God.

No-one can intercede for another. No-one can take the sins of another upon himself. All anyone can do is to point the way, verbally and by example.

Do not make the mistake however, of thinking that memory is just something to be stored against the coming of the judgment day, whether intermediate or final. It is not only that. Now we have it in true perspective, it is seen as something which should be delved into consciously from time to time, as a guide on our true way. For, by an analysis of the memories which make us hot with shame, and those on the other hand which afford satisfaction, we can see more clearly now, if we are working intuitively, the rights and wrongs of past events. Thus, by analyzing our past and relating it to our present, we can in part foresee our future trends and conduct. Then in the light of such analysis, we can start consciously to direct our progress and speed the end of final balance, saving ourselves from much pain and suffering on the way.

Individual memory then, will cease as such when the last earthly body is discarded, and so will individual intuition for we shall be at one with it. The necessity for both will cease. Memory, stripped of its inconsequentials is, seen intuitively, a spiritual guide to error, that is to deviation from intuitional guidance, and so becomes far more important than perhaps we had dreamed of.

Thus, although a man must work out his own salvation, this law of recompense which applies to all he does is not an everlasting treadmill. There is a way out of it which he can find for himself. If, on the other hand, a man has not reached the stage when he wishes to escape from it, he can at least, while continuing to tread it, so conduct his life as to reduce the suffering he must undergo. About one thing there should be no mistake, salvation comes only through suffering. There is no other way. How much suffering there is to be depends upon the individual, for each is the arbiter of his own fate.

The Last Death and Beyond:
The Living Darkness

The number of individuals who reach the last death in any generation is comparatively few. The way is long and arduous and the gate a very narrow one. Indeed it needs to be no wider for salvation is something individual, and the entries are one by one, and even then there is no waiting. One rarely meets another.

The usual time for final identification and illumination, followed by judgment or the day of reckoning, is at or shortly before earthly death, which is then the last bodily death, for the man concerned is now born of the spirit and returns to the flesh no more. In some cases however, when an individual forces the issue, the enlightenment and judgment may occur even fairly early during an earthly life. Then it is as if the man experienced death and what is beyond, and then returned to complete his last earthly existence, for he knows now that after his next death he will not return again. How far he goes is up to the man concerned, for the state of peace and bliss which he finds is not easily interrupted and he is inclined, each time he reaches it, to rest therein. This is the purely individual end, and if this only has been sought, then it may be all before the death of the last body. Life however is never the same as before. The one so purged will never again do evil. He may make mistakes due to the complexity of the superficial life with which he still has to deal, and which, going on all around him, he cannot usually avoid. In matters which are not basic therefore, if he is perhaps rushed for time in complicated artificial matters, he can be in error, which he will realize later and will not repeat. He will always, of course, avoid any such complication if at all possible.

If his bodily or mental health has been afflicted by unconscious worry, fear and frustration, it is possible that some of these conditions may clear up, or at least improve, but deep seated consequences of the law of recompense, mainly group consequences, will generally continue and have to be suffered until the physical end.

If the man concerned, however, has entered this search for Truth motivated by the wish to help others to find it, and knows that, at the present day stage of intellectual development, faith without at least some fair degree of understanding is not possible to a large and rapidly increasing number of people, he will forego the blissful state and will patiently press forward with persistence and humility. Then, sooner or later he will find the knowledge for which he seeks, and a long series of visits will begin. From time to time he will return to The Living Darkness, at peace but nevertheless extremely alert. For although the body and all things material are forgotten, and there is no sight or sound, or anything which can be discerned by bodily sense, The Living Darkness is alive, and he is conscious always of Being. And there, having gone with a mentally prepared question for elucidation, after having taken it to the extreme intellectual end possible for him, he releases it into the void and waits without movement and without thought, held there. After a while, the period varying, he is released and returns to the sights and sounds of daily life. Then again he waits, and at this point in the early stages of his experience sometimes almost despairs, as it seems that his effort has had no result. But gradually, words seep into his mind and he writes, not, it would seem of his own volition, but because he has to do it. Then, after a while, the inspiration ceases and he is left to sort out what has been written. Looking back it is as if, in The Living Darkness, all knowledge is spontaneous and immediate, and it seems as if he is presented with the immediate knowledge of all that was and is, but of which he can only grasp a very little at a time. Absorption of some of this by some method not experienced before takes place, and, after a pause, comes into the mind as words. Sometimes the knowledge acquired in a few minutes, will take hours to re-capture, and years to assimilate. Often he will go without any prepared question but usually, despite this, he will find that he has captured something which can be transmitted to paper. These absorptions and transmissions are of varying lengths, and appear to be quite disconnected, being

42

often on widely different themes. Later however, when a large number are read consecutively, it is found that by re-shuffling, a continuous thread can be distinguished, and followed up by concentrating on it. Questions, however, are not always answered. Sometimes a seeming irrelevant reply comes, but it always has purpose. Sometimes it refers back to a point in the intellectual reasoning made beforehand, and then one returns to what was probably a mistake in reasoning. Then having corrected the sequence, the question may be posed again, this time probably with good results. It is quite useless to attempt to have a question answered unless, first, one's reasoning power and intellectual ability have been used to the very limit of their capacity. Anything less in degree than that will result in complete blankness. One has therefore, a considerable amount of study to do. Retention of all learned from books during this period is however unnecessary and the majority is better dismissed, for as one proceeds further much of it becomes inconsequent and is therefore best forgotten quickly.

So, a man who experiences this comes to know the peace and the bliss which are in God, and he knows, having tested it innumerable times, that in God is all knowledge immediate and available to each man as he returns whence he came. And he realizes now that when he dies he will become, at long last, The One which is God. While in the human frame he can experience this for only short intervals, and for a limited overall period, but he knows without any doubt. So far as is possible in the turmoil of earthly existence, he lives intuitively ever after.

The joy which is in this man, as he is able bit by bit to remove the veils and fathom some of the mysteries is great, and he knows that a half million years of effort have been worth while.

It may be surprising that in all this there is not the slightest sense of loneliness. It will be understood however, when it is realized that loneliness comes of separation and, in The One, is the sense of fulfilment and completion. Here love is lost in the perfect understanding.

It may be and probably is so, that only a few are able to penetrate far enough for any considerable revelation. Every man however, by applying himself persistently and patiently, can find in himself the necessary intuitional guidance, so to direct his life that fear and frustration are overcome, and he can find a true conviction of who and what he really is. Not the fleshy body, not the seething mass of thought, but the serene spiritual entity which awaits identification.

Evil and Sin

Why, it may be asked, should God have allowed evil to develop in the kingdom of man? Why, when man emerged and became the Transition Link between the Natural and Spiritual Phases, should not the change over have been a smooth one, as instinct was gradually replaced by intuition? Evil could then have been avoided, but this would have been at the expense of the independent individual existence of man. There would have been no Psychic Phase. Had this been the case, the whole of The Plan and The Image would have collapsed, because in the first place there would have been no necessity for the faculty of reason (or the breath of life), by means of which man first cut loose from compulsory guidance, and so identified himself as a spiritual being. Some will object and say that the 'breath of life' of the Christian scriptures means the breath or air which keeps alive the physical body. This is not so, the mistake being due to a misinterpretation of the Christian scripture which is dealt with later in the book. The physical body which became man was the same physical body as had been animal and had lived for millions of years in various forms kept alive by the air breathed. The scriptural breath of life which God breathed into man, and into man only, was the spiritual breath of life or the faculty of reason. This it was which made man 'a living soul', that is which allowed the spiritual entity to insulate itself by means of the thought body from return to the original at physical death. Thus it began for the first time a continuous spiritual development independent of physical deaths. And it is the combination of spiritual entity and thought body which is the 'soul'. If this faculty of reason had not been necessary, the physical vehicle or instrument could have been of much less complexity, and, in fact, the whole could have been a conducted tour guided, as it were, by a printed pamphlet of instructions. This would have made the whole of creation absurd. So separation from compulsory guidance had to be.

All sin and all evil comes of separation, and the greater and more complex the separation, the greater and more complex becomes the consequent evil. All started in Unity, in the One-ness of The Absolute Ground, in the (to man), apparent nothingness of the void. Of this was The One without a second, and there was no evil. With the first movement in the void came division, which from the beginning of creation onwards, became increasingly greater. But although division became greater, separation did not, for at the death of any part of creation, however small, the spiritual entity involved returned to the original unity, development being limited in this evolutionary phase to the physical aspect. Only with the formation of the soul of man as a semi-permanent, independent entity did separation increase, for now there was no return at the death of a human physical body. Thus, with the beginning of the soul of man as an independent entity, evil entered creation, for evil is the result of self-conscious self-enhancement, or attempted self-enhancement, of one part at the expense of another or, possibly, many other parts.

In the Natural Phase this cannot be, because progress is, within limits, along the compulsory lines of a plan which was made with an overall view of the whole, and which keeps its balance without the need for conscious direction by any of the individual parts. Moreover the innate tendency of the Natural Phase in all its parts, is for the preservation of species, and the development of new ones as the increasing complexity of the environment demands. It must be remembered that the whole purpose of the Natural Phase is to provide a vehicle and instrument, suitable for breaking away from evolution in order to make the return journey. The whole of this first evolutionary phase therefore, was aimed at this one result, the Transition Link, now accomplished. It was a ruthless competition with many species dying, and others deflecting and new ones arising, until the one arose capable of holding premier place against all competition. That there was competition between indivdiual members within a species, and that the stronger survived while the weaker died, was not because of consciously directed action by one individual against another, but a natural measure in maintaining strength and quality in the species.

This then, was the hereditary atmosphere which passed on with man when he broke loose from the compulsory phase of instinctive guidance, and commenced his own independently guided way. The break was not sudden however, as instinctive guidance faded very slowly at first. Intuitive guidance, intended eventually to take the place of the instinctive, started very slowly as instinct began to fade. So the change over was more or less unnoticeable. The two are bound together and instinct will never be entirely lost until intuitional guidance is complete, which will be when original unity is regained.

As man started on his independently guided existence, the savagery and ruthlessness of self-preservation which was part of the heritage of millions of years of physical development, was still in him. As a self-conscious individual he used this not only for the unconscious purpose of preserving his own species against the competition of all others, but for the conscious purpose of gain to himself, even at the expense of other members of his species. As he increased in numbers and developed mentally, competition with other species became slowly easier, until he had at least temporary dominance over them. Meanwhile he was gaining experience in his independent existence, and beginning to trust more and more to individual decisions aimed at his personal welfare. So in the Psychic Phase he continued to use the instinctive savage and ruthless behaviour which was his heritage from the Natural Phase, but this time mainly against the fellow-individuals of his own species, and in order to forward his personal ends. This savagery and ruthlessness so necessary in the Natural Phase, now came to be used internally in the species Man, both between individuals and groups. So evil started with the commencement of the Psychic Phase when man, as an individual, began to lead an independent existence. And it grew apace, because whereas the savagery and ruthlessness of the animal kingdom had been controlled by the guidance of instinct, man, with his increasing mental development and creative ability, was soon devising means of using his savage inheritance for personal ends unknown before, and with an intensity beyond what was necessary. This was independent man running amuck, and he has continued to do so ever since, particularly as, in the limited view which is all that individual man can see, it appears to help in enhancement of personal well-being. So greater diversity and intensity of evil has come to be, and will continue to increase while man concentrates on himself as an individual personality, the separate existence of which is regarded as an ideal state. From the beginning, so many thousands of years ago man has been separating himself more and more from his source and from his fellow men. His path has been from unity to multiplicity, from simplicity to complexity.

The way back then is apparent. It is a reversal of the process, no longer physically, but mentally and spiritually. The body of man being mortal can return physically, but his spiritual entity is not mortal, and does not die a physical death. When man began to live an independent individual life he became a living soul, a spiritual entity separated from its source by the thought body which he had created, as he used his newly developed reasoning power to break free from the compulsion of the Natural Phase. Each soul then, must continue in individual existence, until it finds its own way back.

Going back to the point where intuition started as the break with instinct was made, we find that instinct was so strong in man that intuition, only then starting its guidance, had difficulty in making itself felt. And this intuition could never do as long as man lived only in the physical body. But now, as an independent entity, he has an independent, continuous existence, and between periods in a physical body, the soul has resting periods out of the body. When a body is discarded, the spiritual entity, now free for a time from all hereditary influence and from instinct and sensory perception, which go with a physical body, is able to see the previous life in retrospect and, being now open to intuition, can evaluate its experience correctly. Thus a re-aligned aim is brought into a new physical existence as a corrective to the much stronger hereditary factors which come with the new fleshy body. This must continue until eventually the re-alignment is complete and the spiritual entity has achieved the reversal, and reduced the multiplicity and complexity of the physical world to the unity

48

and simplicity of the original. When this happens it is once again pure spirit.

Evil, then, starts when the instinctive tendencies which are carried over from the one phase into another, are perverted by the second phase. That is, the tendencies which were natural and necessary with the aims of the Natural Phase, become unnatural and unnecessary in the Psychic Phase, when the aim of the latter is known. The prevalence and increase of evil is due to the general ignorance of the purpose and aim of the second phase, and of the means by which these are realized. Decrease in evil tendencies therefore, can only be accomplished by enlightenment in meaning and purpose.

Simple instinct and intuition are no-thought responses. In the thought (or Psychic) phase however, there is the strong intervention of the mentally reasoned response, which may, too often and too strongly, supersede the Divine direct response.

To sum up, sin is a conscious persistence in error, which is a wrong apprehension of intuitional guidance. Consciousness of error may be given to us by the voice of conscience, or by revelation through prophets and sages, major and minor, throughout the ages, even going back to the most elementary forms of inspiration in primitive man. Also by observation of the results of action.

Evil is misuse of natural forces, and the results of such misuse, due to lack of contact with natural guidance, that is, instinct and/or intuition, to the extent of conscious injury to others, for the sake of the self (whether 'self' be applied to an individual or a group).

Some may view such things as storm and earthquake, famine and disease as evil. These however (excluding the man-made famine and disease of which there is perhaps more than generally realized), are surely what may be called natural hazards.

From the beginning in the Natural Phase of the Earth, there has been a tolerance within limits allowed in all laws, resulting in what we call chance, but what is surely an opportunity for self-direction either by mutation in lesser species, or by deliberate interference with natural law as by man. Such tolerance had to be allowed if Self-revelation was to be accomplished, the alternative of a rigidly preconceived system being limited to initial knowledge. There could not therefore be complete rigidity of detail. This applies locally on Earth and without doubt there is similar limited non-rigidity in the solar and galactic systems. So there is and must always be the chance of occasional calamities, which, as said before, may be called natural hazards. When considering the loss of life occasioned, it should be remembered always that the spiritual man cannot be killed, and victims will soon reincarnate to continue their experience in the physical world.

Outlook on Death

With our realigned beliefs, our attitude towards many events is altered. For instance when we realize that death is only an interlude, and that most of us will live other lives here in the future, which lives will, rightly directed, lead us to the designed end, then the fear of death is overcome. Though this may seem strange at first we soon become accustomed to it. The only ones who have anything to fear from death are the wrong-doers in this present life. Those who put self-consideration before anything else, and live evilly now, have good cause to fear death, since it means for them a step nearer retribution. When reborn again in the flesh, they will suffer in good measure, for make no mistake about it, there is justice in the order of all things. As we sow, so shall we reap, and for many the next life will reveal a sad harvest. So let no-one who is unfortunate in this life complain about it, for it is the result of their past. Not all of it is due to their individual pasts of course, but much of it. And those who, this time, are well-favoured, let them not be over-smug or use their present advantages to the disadvantage of others, for their future lives depend upon their thoughts and actions now.

A word of warning is needed here in case what is said is taken too literally. It is useless simply to do good for one's own sake. Doing it to earn medals, or as the payment of a premium on a next life assurance policy, will be of no avail. The motive must be right before the action can help. In other words, right action must be done for the sake of right action, and not just in the hope of personal benefit.

There is sure to be a sense of loss when a relative or friend dies, and a feeling of sympathy for surviving close relatives. Undue grief however is out of place, for death after a reasonable spell of life is of benefit to the individual, in being an opportunity for re-evaluation and realignment. The death of a young child is usually seen as tragic for the one concerned, whereas it really makes little, if any, difference, for although its life has been cut short, if the waiting period before its rebirth is correspondingly reduced, nothing is lost. Any undue show of grief is to be deprecated. The spiritual entity concerned has entered upon a stage which cannot be affected in any way by anything human beings may do. The remaining shell, the empty body of the flesh, is already on its way back to the dust of the earth and the atmosphere, from which, in due course, other physical bodies will be made. All that remains to be done therefore, is to dispose decently of this shell, in and by means of which the spiritual entity was able to live in the physical world, and add another chapter to its book of experience. Unnecessary show and expense at the funeral cannot be of any use to the departed one. This is usually a display of pride, or a sign of undue attachment to, sometimes amounting almost to worship of, the physical body. It shows a lack of understanding on the part of those concerned.

Those who have lost dear ones due to what are called unnatural means, as for instance in accidents or murder, should remember that it is not possible to kill the spiritual entity, and it is only the body which dies, and which in due course will be replaced by another. Sorrow for the sufferings before death, though natural perhaps, should be overcome as soon as possible, for to indulge in it without check is harmful to one's own outlook and progress, which can thus be considerably unbalanced.

Sometimes, particularly in the case of chronic invalids, one will hear it said that death came as a blessing. This is true but such an attitude must be adopted cautiously, for suffering particularly when prolonged, may be a great refining influence, or when intense for a comparatively short period, can sometimes bring a person closer to truth than might have been achieved otherwise in a lifetime.

Those who aim to prolong indefinitely periods of human life on earth are wrong. They are wrong firstly because bodily death is, as has been pointed out before, a natural break in the total earth life of a man, during which, undisturbed by the physical body and senses, the spiritual entity may readjust its aims and realign its progress for the future. Secondly, if the unnatural prolongation of life in the flesh is suggested or attempted because of fear of what follows, then this new outlook should remove the fear, and therefore the necessity for or desirability of, the prolongation. Such prolongation would, in fact, delay the progress of the one involved if his present alignment was not correct.

Children

The outlook on children changes as we adjust to the new frame of belief. The fleshy body of the child comes of the sexual union of the human father and mother. In the child they become one flesh. They have no part however, in the production of the spiritual entity which inhabits the material body for a term on earth. This, as we have seen before, is an immortal everlasting entity, and the life on earth which commences in a particular child, is one of a long series through which the entity passes. The human mother and father, although they have not contributed to the spiritual entity before birth, do however contribute to its future, for they pass on through the flesh hereditary traits which may greatly affect the life of the child. These combine with spiritual tendencies carried forward in the spiritual entity or soul and, together with external environment, may act as checks or encouragements in certain directions. So the mother and father give to the entity a temporary human habitation, and a temporary name, together with certain hereditary tendencies, but they are not in any way responsible for the previous spiritual development. For in the spirit are no mothers and fathers or the need for them. The only ancestors of the soul is itself in its previous incarnations in the flesh, and it is from them that it brings certain tendencies to this new incarnation. So, then, a tremendous range in variations of experience of individuals is the outcome of the various combinations of large numbers of physical and spiritual tendencies, and a large variety also of external environmental conditions. These can result in anything from genius in one to half-wittedness in another, from buoyant health to life-long sickness and so on. The particular combination experienced by a soul is approximately correct in the long view, for a right alignment of progress. Approximate because it is within limits, and the tolerance allowed permits a man to adjust his progress to a certain extent, thus consciously assisting in the creation of his own intermediate destinies. If general hereditary tendencies are sufficiently

54

retrograde to overcome the progressive spiritual tendency, then the general progress and development may slow down while frustration and suffering increases. It is therefore incumbent upon parents to pass on the best possible hereditary conditions.

Many parents may find answers here to puzzling questions which have often arisen in their minds. For instance, why are two of their children so different in behaviour and outlook? Or why is one so intelligent while the other is, maybe, inept? Why should one be physically handicapped while another has perfect health? Why are children so often very different from their parents? And so on.

In most cases, there are good reasons behind such handicaps, which are part of a very long process extending far back into the past and on into the future. So parents should not grieve overmuch but should co-operate realistically in helping the handicapped soul on its journey. They will blame themselves only if, in full knowledge of what they were doing, and knowing it to be avoidable, they have passed on to their children unfavourable hereditary conditions or poor early spiritual guidance.

It may be difficult at first for parents to realize that their child is only, if the term may be used, semi-related to them, in other words that they are responsible only for providing the fleshy frame. It must be realized however, that it is the cloying, over-emotional ties which many parents think should exist between them and their children throughout their lives, which go far in checking real spiritual progress. It is a case of the flesh obscuring the spirit, and can cause much unhappiness. Those parents are wise who, before having children, adjust their outlook so that they do not expect too much of love or gratitude from their offspring. Do not expect gratitude from a child because you produced it, because you feed and clothe it decently, or because you give it a good education. As always it is the motivation which counts, and how many parents can say truthfully that they had a child for the sake of that child, and because they thought the child would like it? Usually a baby is conceived due to an innate urge in the parents. It may be from choice because they wish to become parents, or it may be accidentally, but it is a rare case for conception to be due to consideration for the unborn. This being so, why should gratitude be expected from children? They are entited to what you can give them. Admittedly some receive from their parents more than others. Usually however a child will notice this for itself, and will respond naturally if gratitude is not drummed into it ad nauseam. A child has a right to expect good treatment from its parents until it can fend for itself. This treatment will, or should, include guidance in things material and spiritual. The child also has a right, when it is of a sufficient intelligence to make decisions for itself, to expect a lessening of pressure from its parents. The duty of the latter is no less in ceasing to give, than in giving, to children. They should never forget that, when the initial physical and mental training of a child has reaccustomed the soul to its material surroundings, it then starts to redevelop spiritually, and here is the crux; it may be older in experience, and more developed spiritually, than either of its parents. A choir-boy may be spiritually more mature than a bishop. Not all present human beings became human at the same time or have progressed at the same rate, and the earlier and more experienced may quite often be born of later and less experienced parents, although as a rule this will not be apparent until the necessary readjustment to the physical world has been made.

Parents who constantly reiterate the need for gratitude on the part of a child, should be careful, for a child is very alert and will, at a comparatively early age, see through this attitude to the true motivation of its being here, with a consequent loss of respect for its parents.

A child has, nevertheless, a duty towards its parents, and if relationships are unforced, and depend rather on truth and justice than on over-emotional ties, friendship will probably develop which will lead to a natural return of good offices to the helpless as the years go by. For as the physical bodies of the children are nurtured when helpless in youth, it is the physical bodies of the parents which must be tended in later years, and as the first is the duty of the parents, so is the second the duty of the children. As for instance Jesus on the cross who, admitting responsibility for his mother, passed it on, saying to the disciple, 'Behold thy mother! And from that hour that disciple took her into his own home.' (John, xix, 27.) So always give children affection, justice and truth, but expect nothing in return. They are happy parents who then find, later in life, that they have the affectionate friendship of their children. This they are more likely to have, than if they have tried to form and maintain strict emotional ties with their children. Moreover they will have assisted their own spiritual progress, for it is the ones who are nearest to us, who most obscure the truth. Jesus knew this and said :

'For I am come to set a man at variance against his father, and the daughter against her mother, and the daughter-in-law against her mother-in-law. And a man's foes shall be they of his own household. He that loveth father and mother more than me, is not worthy of me; and he that loveth son and daughter more than me, is not worthy of me.' (Matt. x, 35-37.)

This sets the fleshy and emotional ties to relatives against the spiritual ties to God, and says that the emotional outlook must not be allowed to obscure the tie of first importance, that to God, and veil the truth that affinity to Him is greater than it is to the family.

The bonds of the flesh are strong in the human being, but if they are too strong, they can hide the truth, so that man identifies himself completely with the fleshy body. The real and abiding entity in a man does not derive from his father and mother, is not of their making or choosing. The temporary habitation of their making is mortal and when finished with, will end as, and in, material. A man must realize the transience of the bonds of the flesh, and break through the emotions to see what he truly is. His first duty is to the source of his spiritual self, and the fleshy ties must be subordinated to this.

Jesus said to his mother, 'Woman, what have I to do with thee? mine hour is not yet come'. (John ii, 4.) A clear indication that, until the hour of his release from the flesh, his mother had no further responsibility towards, or hold on, him. When the hour came, then the fleshy body which she had borne could be returned to her. The bond between them was of the flesh.

So, when a child is to be brought into the world, selfish motives should become secondary and, before the child is conceived, the minds of the parents should be prepared to accept it as something less than their very own, something more than a being to be developed on lines to suit their dictates and preferences, something which, after initial care and guidance, is to be freed from obligation, free to choose as it will. Above all the conception of a child must be thought of as being the opportunity for a soul which is waiting to further its spiritual progress. And, before anyone may be tempted to neglect their duty to children, or to treat the matter in any way lightly, it should be remembered that before long, someone will be having to do the same for them again, and they in their turn will be to some extent dependent upon these others for help in their own progress.

Prayer

Anthropomorphism of God, or the imagining of God as an out-size man, and prayer to Him, are devices to suit a limited conception of God, and are therefore only of use in the early stages of the search for Truth. As God is conceived more as a power than as a person, then approach to It becomes more the silent achievement of an elevated plane of consciousness, than a matter for word or thought.

Sincere individual prayer, particularly in a time of stress or complete frustration, can raise the consciousness temporarily above the thought level, with greater intuitive understanding of problems and consequent greater strength to deal with them. This state cannot be maintained and the normal level is resumed. In retrospect it appears as if the prayer had resulted in help from an outside source.

If then the eventual aim be that prayer is known, not as words or thoughts, but as a conscious attempt to overcome them, so as to produce the opening in the thought barrier, through which the spirit may rise momentarily to a glimpse of Truth, this is good. If however, prayer be known as an attempt to pull spirit down, then it is not good. God must not stoop. Man must soar.

Man is essentially a self-sufficient being. It is the realization of this which is so difficult. Eventually all will realize that a man must prepare himself to take what is, and not ask to be prepared to receive it as a gift. For That which man really is, prepared in the beginning for Itself that which man can find and take for himself. When man realizes this with conviction, he uses the guidance which is and always has been there for him to use, to return to That.

If, in the early stages, a man must pray in word and thought, there is nothing wrong with his praying to the God immanent within him so long as he realizes that he is really praying to his own greater self, the undying spiritual entity from everlasting. For a man who is unaware, this is a separate self from his present

59

realized self, which he identifies with his body and brain. Pent up emotion can be released to that inner entity. And great strength can be found in appeal to it, and in communion with it, for there exists nothing closer to a man than this, the Immanent God awaiting recognition. This only applies while a man identifies himself with the body. After his enlightenment, when he has identified himself completely with this greater self, he becomes the Son of God and then, if he prays, he will pray to the Transcendent. Thus the ratio remains the same, man to Immanent God, and Son of God to Transcendent God.

It should be understood that there is no duality here. There is in man only the one entity or self, but it has a dual outlook.

Lust for Power

In the beginning all was latency, all power was on leash, and there was no movement in The Void. In the very first movement came an opening up of the latency, but the power, although now operating, was still on leash and controlled. And throughout the whole Natural Cycle this remains so, it being controlled, not by an external source operating independently, but by an inherent affinity for the regulations or laws laid down in The Plan. And the Natural Cycle will continue so until, eventually, it returns to its first state. From the beginning tolerance was allowed in the regulations, which permits of deviation from them within limits. In man however, arrives a creature which is able to leave the strict regulations of the evolutionary cycle, and determine its own course. Thus arises a dangerous situation, for the entity which is man, and which now commences an independent continuous development, is a spiritual entity, a unit of The Intelligence, The Creator. And in it is the inherent knowledge of its great power. Combined with this is, suddenly, the realization that it is not only an individual member of its species, but an individual personality, different from every other of its species, and conscious of obstruction by, and interference from, others in attaining its desires. So the power of the individual is used for the personal ends of the single entity, independent of the laws. In other words, power is off the leash for the first time, and each unit with its modicum of power, uses it for its personal ends or, as necessary, grouping and using it first for group and then for national ends. All this is without an overall view of The Plan, so that Power runs amuck without true aim or guidance. As a result personal or group ends are deemed of more importance than the combined ultimate end, which is mainly not known at all. And, although he does not generally realize it, the further man drives from the guidance, either instinctive or intuitive, the greater his suffering will become.

So man has now another urge which will not be gainsaid, in

addition to the compulsive sexual urge. And this one is even more dangerous, for whereas the sexual urge operates individually, this urge or lust for power is not only individual but can be combined, and thus increased in potency until it is something frightful. Moreover, whereas sexual lust usually decreases or even ceases, with bodily age, this is not the same with lust for power. This can continue and intensify up to the bodily death of the individual, and, in the case of groups, is often independent of individual deaths. So Lust for Power must be regarded as the main enemy, with Sexual Lust secondary to it.

Indivisibility of God

Much of what has been said already, may give some the impression of a belief in the divisibility of God. Such is not the case. The difficulty is in attempting to give the slightest idea of what God is, when It can only be realized in union. It would be easier to attempt to find a no-dimensional, non-existent spot in space, than to attempt to describe what only is. Yet something must be attempted to try and correct any impression given of divisibility. So, with the difficulties understood, just a few words of attempt at explanation.

When it is said that there is a spiritual entity in the every part and particle of creation, this would seem to suggest a division of God. Perhaps to imagine God as an immense ocean will help, with all the separate entities as drops of spray, leading short independent existences, some larger than others, as droplets encased in their individual skins or casings. After a very short time they fall back into the ocean. During their independent existences, the entities are not really any less of the ocean than when combined with it, nor is the ocean any less an ocean because of the constant spray.

The likeness should stop there, because to take it any further would be wrong, as spray is external to the ocean, whereas the spiritual entities are not external to God. It is only after hesitating for a long time that this attempt has been made. Please do not carry it too far in any direction, for it is already wrong, and to go any further would be only to go further wrong. Another very tentative attempt, is to imagine all these spiritual entities as cells of the mind of God at work in the body of God. There we go again—body—sufficient to start most people imagining a shape again. So you see the difficulty. But perhaps this may be of some assistance.

Do not imagine God as a body of any kind whatsoever. Even anything so tenuous as a body of thought is not even to be considered. Nor any shape, nor any form, nor any substance, nor any nature whatsoever. The East is right when it says that any attempt at description of The One can only be by negatives. It is not this, or that, or the other. No-one will ever get nearer than that.

Even when merging is accomplished nothing nearer is possible, for then there is nothing else.

Love

Considering the type of book this is, it may surprise some that little mention is made of love. There are several reasons.

Love is strictly applicable to a person or individuality. It does not apply to that final state of unity which transcends personality and individuality. Love is a giving out of the spiritual entity towards, or an act of coming to oneness with, or in other words, a coming to a complete spiritual understanding of.

The love of self is turned to love of God in degree, only as the self in man is identified with the spiritual entity in man, which is Immanent God. And the self of man as man, can never identify itself with Transcendent God. Only Immanent God can do that. And man only becomes Immanent God when his identification with the Immanent God is complete. Love of The Transcendent, by man as man, is impossible of accomplishment.

There is no objection to the use of the term as true disinterested charity, which is unchanging and regardless of object. Disinterested charity (for charity read service rather than alms giving), is dependent on a coming to oneness with the object, even though in degree.

All other forms of love are dependent on their object and therefore, although some forms may be, in degree, good, they are all suspect.

The word as used loosely by so many today can be misleading, and is better avoided altogether.

When it is used in a connection overmuch concerned with sex or sexual desire or appetite, by those who are in complete, or almost complete, submission to the dictates of the physical body and senses, it is but to travesty that which is holy, and is a sign of spiritual blindness, and a self-blinded man of such description cannot know love.

There should not be any mistake here. What was said in the last paragraph does not mean that love between man and woman should not include the sexual impulse. In true love between a man and a woman the sexual act can become holy in its being an approach to the true spiritual 'coming to oneness'.

One other reason for the word being suspect is that Christianity is over-loaded with it due to the general over-emotional outlook, and avoidance of it may therefore help as a corrective tendency.

No Hell for Animals

Hell, or this place of trial and suffering, is a combined physical and psychic state. It is a product of the thinking and reasoning which severed man from the Natural Phase, and made him an independent entity. So it is a consequence of independence. Comparatively suddenly, man has had to assume conscious responsibility for his actions, and since then the hellish brew of uncertainty, fear and frustration, which simmered only slowly at first will soon be boiling. For man has almost lost connection with guidance of any sort or, rather, he mainly disregards it. Instead of all his actions being without responsibility, as they were when he was in the animal kingdom, now nearly every action he takes is self-directed and the responsibility of it being right or wrong is directly upon him. On the other hand he has no sure belief in the why and wherefore of life, for the continuing guidance of intuition has not been cultivated, has in fact been mainly shunned, in the short-sighted belief that personal benefit derived from such an attitude. So, adrift from the safety of the past, he is afraid of the future. Disease, starvation, war, all stare him in the face, and with no secure sense of a future after death, he turns more and more to the pleasures of the moment, to the cult of bodily satisfaction in the present, no matter at whose expense it may be.

When individual man again approaches the condition of acting without consideration of result, that is as nearly as possible wholly intuitionally, then his hell subsides, for it is mainly mental. The physical aspect still remains as he still shares in group consequences but, with the majority of the mental load removed, his hell becomes comparatively easy to bear.

The physical consequences alone can be unpleasant, but it is anticipating them as an inevitable part of life in the flesh, without being able to see reason or justice in them which causes the mental load. Add to these the ever increasing anticipation and dreads of the future, and the frustration and helplessness he feels in that he can see neither meaning nor purpose in it all, and he is really in his hell.

Animals are spared most of this.

It is true that they suffer pain but, comparatively, if they are left alone in a completely natural state, the pain is short lived. For instance, an animal badly wounded by accident or attack will feel pain, but only for a comparatively short period, for it will either recover fairly soon, as it must if it is to find food, or it will die fairly soon because it cannot find food, due to its injuries. Either way the period is not protracted. If anyone should think that death by starvation is extremely painful, they should try, (under supervision), a complete fast with nothing but water, for seven days. They will find that after the first few days are over, the desire for food declines, and after a few more it is sometimes necessary almost to force oneself to eat. This plus a weakened state due to say loss of blood, brings a fairly quick and easy end. In the animal kingdom a natural death is very often due to starvation, for when the old animal can no longer find its food, it submits quietly to the inevitable. It knows nothing of a possible future life. It knows nothing of sin or consequences or need of forgiveness. It has no anticipation of a protracted period of suffering. It has no mental suffering at all nor the need for it, unless this enters in slight degree in the higher forms. All its life it has submitted to a guiding instinct, and when the guiding instinct prompts it to lie down and die quietly, it does so, in faith if you like, in the instinct. There is no hell in this. Man would be very happy to do the same. Some do, but not many.

Another way in which animals die is of course the, to us, horrifying way of being killed and eaten as food by other animals. Remember first that although fighting takes place between the individuals of a species, this does not on the whole usually result in death. Animals killed by others for food obviously suffer pain, but it is usually short lived and is physical only. And, as we go down the scale from higher to lower animal life, sensitivity to physical pain as we know it apparently becomes less. But the main difference perhaps, is that there is little or no anticipation. And pain is in the mind. You need only to cut, or anaesthetize, the link between body and mind and you can cut the body up without pain being felt. And dread comes of thinking. Any comparatively minor hell which may be experienced by some animals is often of man's making.

And remember too, that if life in the Natural Phase had been completely idyllic, the break with it might have been made with greater reluctance. Still more likely is, that the climb out of it would have been slowed down, if not stopped altogether, for a comparison with what had been left, and what was developing, would have been so much more in favour of the Natural, that Psychic development could have been slowed down indefinitely or stopped.

It will be seen that, in addition to the scientifically realized balance in all the Natural Phase, which man can so easily upset in some of its aspects, there is a further balance which is perhaps not generally realized, between beauty and ugliness. There has to be. If life in all its aspects in the Natural and Psychic Phases was of extreme beauty, with none of the ugliness of catastrophe and disease, of cruelty and dread, of frustration and remorse, spiritual return to the source would be checked or altogether stopped. If, on the other hand, the ugliness of life were demonstrated over-much relative to the beautiful, then man would not wish to remain long enough to fulfil the purpose of his being here, and would try to take his own way out of it.

It may then be felt that animals have to suffer for the sake of man. But do not forget that God, in degree, is in both man and animal, so basically it is God suffering for the self-revelation of God.*

* See page 70—'The Indwelling Entity'.

The Indwelling Entity

It is not claimed, anywhere in this book, that the belief expressed is only on amalgam of parts of the beliefs of the various great religions. More than once it is stated that, in addition to such an amalgam, there is original material added which derived from the revelation. Moreover, in the introduction it was requested that, for the time taken to read this book, readers would dismiss any present belief they held and read if possible with a completely open mind. However, this being very difficult, it is certain that there will be objection raised to one aspect of this belief in particular. That is, that the unit of Immanent God in a human being is subject to the dichotomy of joy and sorrow, love and hate etc. It is generally believed that the serene indwelling spiritual entity is above such. If this were so then there must be a second entity which is subject to the conditions of the physical world and sees, hears and feels through the medium of the physical sensory system. In this case, at the time of enlightenment, the second entity would need to merge with the first and then later the first, or Immanent God, would need to merge with The Transcendent. The belief in this book maintains that such is not the case. There is a single entity only in man, a unit of Immanent God. This unit is in all living things, conditioned in fulfilment of The Plan, and it is temporarily subject to all the conditions of the Natural and Psychic Phases. It experiences the whole of creation in pursuance of the original end of opening up the latency and revealing It to Itself. It must do this or it could not, during its independent development in man, extend the original creation in the opening up process. This is what hell is. The state in which the separated Immanent God is temporarily subservient to physical creation, and salvation or enlightenment is the means of release. This does not clash with the belief of some religions that there is a hell after this life which we are living. Of course there is for the next physical life we live is a further hell, and so is each until we

70

release ourselves from the need for further experience in the flesh.

This single individual entity therefore has, during its continuous development in man, a dual outlook, one on a higher level than the other. While subject to the overpowering conditions of the material world, it cannot maintain a constant outlook on the higher level and indeed, this outlook is often almost completely lost. Even when, in the later stages of development the high level is found more often and for longer periods, it is still subject, to the very end of physical existence, to being pulled down from the higher to the lower level. Jesus, on the cross, despite his almost unbroken maintenance of higher outlook, was still at the end pulled down by the last kick of the Natural Phase through the pain from the physical body, 'My God, My God, why hast thou forsaken me?' Immanent God finds complete freedom and serenity as it merges with Transcendent God, but not until the last physical body is discarded can this become a permanent state.

This spiritual unit has the inherent knowledge of all that is in reality, and on the other hand it sees, hears and feels through the physical sensory system. It equates, compares, decides, makes mistakes and generally slowly progresses. It is the only entity which uses the physical body and brain to decide its problems, implement its decisions and gradually progress towards its inevitable end.

The soul commences in man. It is not, in this belief, the purely spiritual entity alone. It is that entity with its insulating thought body which arises first in man. At the death of all living things below man, the spiritual entity returns to its original state but in the Psychic Phase in man, for the first time, it is insulated by the thought body when it leaves the dead physical envelope, and it goes on through many lives in a continuous spiritual development. Thus when the soul is spoken of in this book, it means the spiritual entity complete with its insulating envelope or thought body, a new one being formed in each physical life, the old one being discarded at rebirth.

The collective entity which gradually develops and works through its own creation is the suffering Immanent God, unaware or only dimly conscious most of the time, of its origin. It gradually fights through, unit by unit, to its former state of Transcendence.

The spiritual entity in a man then, is a unit of Immanent God, travelling with the aid of a Self-evolved instrument, along a Self-developed path, through the blindness of a Self-inflicted but necessary handicap, with the aid of Self-preprovided intuitive guidance, to a Self-preimaged end, for the sake of Self-revelation.

It is all a becoming. A gradual development with the aid of inherent knowledge of The Image. Or, if you can accept an extreme view, we may be seen as cells in the mind of God working a thought of God through to fruition, becoming one with the thinker again as the process ends.

If occasionally in the book the term 'the little self', is used, it is figurative only, indicating the lower outlook, and should not be taken as meaning a separate entity.

Sleep

The results of recent scientific experiments make it quite clear that dreams are essential to the well being of the human. If an individual is prevented from dreaming he becomes unbalanced. Sleep, of itself, is not the answer. It is accompanying dreams, remembered or not, which maintain the balance.

This is particularly interesting because years ago (incidentally before the publication of the above results), when revelation came by way of query and answer in periods of meditation, an answer stands out in memory very sharply. The question was, 'What is the purpose of sleep?' And the answer, clear cut and immediate, 'To refresh the soul'.

That it also rests the body is undeniable, but this seems to be a secondary consideration unless the body has been worked at a rate above its reasonable capacity.

Medical opinion has been given that, neglecting the mind, the healthy body as a mechanism/organism could continue to work unceasingly. Whether or not it would wear out more quickly is beside the point, although it probably would not if sufficient periods of physical relaxation were allowed, that is relaxation without the accompanying unconsciousness of sleep. And after all much of it, respiratory, circulatory and digestive organs, do continue to function without cessation. This tends to confirm that the primary purpose of sleep is not on account of the body.

It is at least sure that the very tired soul which so often seeks refuge in sleep, awakens refreshed and lightened of much of its load, unless something unusual prevents this. There seems little doubt that the spiritual entity, in its conditioned state as the human soul, needs these frequent breaks from the overwhelming evidence of the physical senses and accompanying thought, in order to balance these impressions with intuitional guidance.*

Sleep is perhaps comparable to a little death during which, away from sense impressions, intuition can be brought to bear on

* See 'The Indwelling Entity' on page 70.

the memory of the previous day's activities as a small alignment, which would account for the good often experienced by what is called 'sleeping on a problem'. There are differences, for it seems that whereas memory of one life is wiped out before rebirth in another, excepting possibly in cases such as early death and quick rebirth, memory remains when reawakening from sleep. This is accounted for however by the fact that the memory of a single day which may be reviewed during sleep, is still required for the combined review after death, whereas the total life memory which is reviewed in the waiting period before rebirth, is not required again for the new life. This is because the spiritual impression taken into a new life by the soul, goes into a different heredity, and is influenced by different general environmental factors than applied in the previous life, whereas in sleep these two factors remain the same on reawakening. So there is a difference, that is, continuity of memory, between the little death, or sleep, and the main death. Also of course that the same physical body survives the one but not the other. It is strange really, considering the similarity between the two states, that we should so welcome the one, and yet be so afraid of the other. It is only because we are unable to see the continuity of the bigger one, until we have transcended the physical hold.

It is a known fact that problems of all sorts can be solved during sleep, the answers being often of an inspirational type, and also that inspirational prose and verse can be found and, as it were, written in the memory for recall when sleep is over. It is therefore clear, at least to those who have experienced these things, that the mind is active at least part of the time during sleep, and that, due to the often inspirational nature of the results, it has been more closely in contact with intuition than is usual in the waking state. A similar condition in the waking state is, in fact, only achieved by complete relaxation of the body and mind, and the stoppage of all thought. It seems obvious therefore, that intelligent use of the sleeping state can be of importance to us. Great care however is needed to avoid becoming unbalanced through mistaking as inspirational, dreams which are not so.

In the experiments mentioned at the beginning of this chapter the electrical impulses of the brain were recorded and the pattern of these during dream periods was quite different from the pattern of the remaining periods. As there were only the two patterns mentioned, the implication seems to be that the non-dream pattern must include all other activity than dreams. As it is quite certain that there is other activity, it follows therefore, that there is never a cessation of it unless, in all the experiments undertaken no other activity whatsoever took place in any of the subjects. As the number of experiments was large this seems unlikely. On the other hand, if the non-dream pattern is considered to indicate a period of non-activity, then it remains to be accounted for how activity other than dreaming was not indicated on the meters, unless of a nature which cannot be so registered.

It is quite possible to use the mind with conscious direction during sleep. When it has become accustomed to concentration on set thought sequences during waking hours, the time comes when, if this is done just before one falls asleep, and the last question of the sequence is carried forward into the sleeping state with a request for enquiry, it will often be found that the solution to a problem or the answer to a query etc., will be present in the mind on awakening. Indeed it sometimes occurs that if the matter is one which has been regarded as urgent, one is awakened with the answer at any time during the night. It is therefore prudent to have paper and pencil handy at all times, otherwise the answer may be completely lost.

Incidentally, when you are able, lying down, to relax the body and consciously to stop all thought, you will find sleep comes almost immediately, unless for some reason you remain alert and prevent it.

Sleep walking is a condition which must be fitted in to the general picture. It seems to provide evidence that eyes and hands are not the only means of guidance through fairly intricate patterns of furniture etc., without touching any, and up and down flights of stairs. That something guides the body is certain, particularly when climbing through an upstairs window and safely back again is included in a walk, something which had never been done before when asleep or awake, and was not therefore due to familiarity or habit. These were experiences of the writer in his young days, and always when told quietly by his father to, 'Go back to bed', he would retrace his steps exactly, return to bed, and have no memory of it on awakening.

Obviously in the foregoing the sense of hearing was alert or he would not have responded to the order to 'Go back to bed'. How complete a severance from the physical sense of touch is achieved at times, however, is instanced by another experience of the writer.

One night his father, hearing a noise in the next (the writer's) bedroom, came to the door of the room and opened it quickly and rather violently until unexpectedly stopped by something behind it. The quick violent opening was due to his father being afraid, because this was shortly after the occasion in which the writer had climbed out of the window. The object behind the door proved to be the writer, standing fast asleep. Told to go back to bed, he did so without waking, and it was only while he was doing so that his father noticed that both his large toes were bleeding. He then awakened the writer and the toes were attended to. One toe was worse than the other, but both nails had been lifted upward and torn from the flesh by the force of the opening door. The whole point here is that, until awakened, the writer knew nothing of the incident and had felt no pain whatsoever, although this was felt immediately on awakening. This shows how far we can withdraw from physical sensation while still in the body. Strangely however, in this case, although nothing was felt, the quietly spoken order 'Go back to bed', registered and was acted upon.

From the beginning this subject of sleep has been a difficult one. Even the first answer 'To refresh the soul', was puzzling because at first it was not realized what constituted the soul, and also it was thought that the primary purpose of sleep was bodily recuperation. Later on further attempts to delve into the sleeping and dreaming states met with unusual resistance. After returning fitfully to the subject from time to time for seven years without further satisfaction, it suddenly seems to be settled and, appropriately enough, this conviction came in the middle of the night, and this paragraph and those following were hurriedly scribbled in a short waking interlude.

It has proved so extraordinarily difficult because, once it had been established that the basic short term purpose of these states was in maintaining a balanced outlook and progressive alignment, than any further detailed investigation is mainly of a psychic nature and therefore out of place in this book. Moreover the deliberate technique of solving problems during sleep has been followed only occasionally for some years. Many solutions have been received spontaneously during sleep but not of deliberate intent and aforethought because, remembering the primary purpose, it seems evident that overmuch deliberate direction of the mind in sleep should be avoided, otherwise the primary purpose might be interfered with to the detriment of the individual.

The main purpose of this book is a spiritual search and anything else is incidental. An attempt at detailed investigation of psychic phenomena would be out of place and, moreover, could prove over-absorbing. Thus it could easily become another of the side lines such as Spiritualism, Faith Healing etc., and be both time wasting and, if taken seriously, might eventually obscure the main end.

Transition Link:
From Risen Ape to God

The so-called little self is with us all the time, a product of the savage rise through the animal kingdom. It was there when we passed over what we may call the border to the start of human status. It was there because it had to be to assure the predesigned end. But, having achieved human status, and having become conscious of that little self and of an alternative to it, preservation and enhancement of it is not now necessary and is indeed harmful.

It must be remembered that the way back is eventually a complete reversal of the way out, and this includes reversing obsessions with territorial rights, social scales etc., which were with us as we crossed the border, and are now pushed to unwarrantable extremes.

It must never be forgotten that the only thing God made in perfection was the Mind Image. Physical creation commenced in the extreme raw state, and has to rise to the only thing created in perfection, that is The Image and it is in man, The Transition Link, that the reversal is made. Put all ideas of a special creation in the physical world behind you therefore, and concentrate on the necessary reversal, which is the only way of achieving the climax of The Plan. Put your trust in God but also, for God's sake, help yourselves. If you don't no one else will. The saying that God helps those who help themselves is true, and without the help of yourselves you can expect none from God. You have cut free from the comparatively easy way of compliance with compulsive directives, and your way temporarily is in general as planned by yourself, with only the remnants of the old guidance and the dawnings of the new to help. But the new is there and is strong if heeded. If we offend by refusal of it, as we do when we take no heed of real meaning and purpose, and when we refuse to help ourselves, we shall be and are individually cut off, and shall so remain until we seek our own salvation in the intended way, and with the predesigned and inherent help which is always there waiting to be found.

We came up the hard way without any special dispensation and, although the Transition Link was planned, it was free competition from the beginning, but always under laws with limits of tolerance which allowed for what is called chance. Mutations, after all, are surely a precaution against unforeseen circumstances which must always arise if complete rigidity is to be avoided, and complete rigidity would be in opposition to original purpose. We became special only when insulation of the unit spiritual entity from God by the thought body, that is with the coming into being of the soul, made the continuous development of an individual spiritual entity possible. Our species happened to be the one to break through. If we had not, then a mutation of some other species would have done so.

Instinct is the response to the natural laws which have existed from the start of creation, laws which ensure procedure along lines which lead towards The Image. It varies according to species and to the plane of consciousness on which they are at any time, just as intuition varies in the human according to development, or, if you will, to the plane of consciousness. We won the competition, other animal species being our competitors in the race, the nearer ones our cousins, and they should be treated as such. That some found blind ends in over specialization etc., and that others ran us close but were somewhat slower, was their misfortune. Someone had to win. It happened to be us.

God's plan required a species sufficient to the purpose of transition. He did not create The Image in the fullness of detail. He was not concerned whether the final species had two arms or three, two noses or one. He required a species which could dominate all others and hold pride of place against all comers. One which could secure the reversal of direction, in which the individual spiritual entity could develop, and from which it could return to the source. Any religious belief which suffers from anthropomorphism does so because of the misconception that God, in imagining man in His likeness, did so in detail including physical

79

characteristics, whereas in God is no shape and no form and nothing physical whatsoever. Man as the Transition Link was created in The Image in the spiritual likeness of God, without reference to physical shape, size, or form. Man, at the apex of physical development and evolution is over-proud in his premier place, forgetting or not knowing that he is still only beginning the necessary spiritual development and evolution which must end in the naughting of all which is physical.

This book reveals that when the individual spiritual entity in man began to develop, true man emerged from the ranks of the animal or near-man. In Biblical language man, receiving the 'breath of life', became 'a living soul'. It is interesting to see how far this equates with science. It is known that the primate brain increased in size very, very slowly and gradually, for about seventy million years. Then, in a comparatively short time, it suddenly almost trebled in size. It seems a reasonable assumption that the commencement of this sudden increase coincided with that of the continuous spiritual development of the soul, both these coming with the emergence of man, there being no such continuous spiritual development in the animal kingdom proper. In other words, the physical instrument evolved through the Natural Phase becomes suitable for development by the spiritual entity in the next or Psychic Phase, for the purpose of breaking down the physical/sensous/instinctive obstruction to the ultimate end of freed spirit.

To one obsessed by the purely evolutionary aspect of the universe and its inhabitants, man no doubt seems to be mathematically improbable. To one who believes that underlying evolutionary progress there is the law and order, always with limits of tolerance, of an overall predesigned plan and purpose, the Transition Link which man is, is a mathematical certainty. Luck has not been the over-riding factor in his gene manipulation. The arrival at the physical climax surely, was the easier part of The Plan to achieve, for underlying all is the inherent pull of the lines to The Image as a guide. There is not even a suspicion of an alternative way to confuse one. The more difficult part must be in the reversal and return, as the path to be taken is against all previous trends, and means the conscious breaking down of all previous knowledge and experience. For the life of man is still ruled largely by animal instincts which he inherited, and man is still very young and very proud in his new estate.

Man still lives regulated far more by the results of instinct than he generally realizes, and this is a part of the blindfold which has to be removed. He must come to understand better what is instinctive and what in and of him is a result of it. He will find that much of what he deems important to him today is due to it. Then he must come to see that it is just this, the necessary guidance through the Natural Phase which, carried into the next, or Psychic Phase, causes most of the trouble and sorrow which is the lot of mankind today. For instinctive guidance is related to the physical vehicle, and is neither appropriate nor intended for use in the phase from the natural to the spiritual. It must be broken down and intuitional guidance, relevant to the spiritual end must take its place. Until this is done and the results of the instinctive urge through the Natural Phase, which have been projected into the present Psychic Phase, are seen intuitively as out of place and wrong, mankind will continue to suffer more and more, for men only continue to extend these results further and further and aggravate the confusion. There must be a real opening of the eyes, a real understanding of the ultimate end in view, and a real and clear conception of what man is, and where in the overall scheme he stands at present. Then there must be a concerted drive away from the present blind and distorted extension of what is instinctive, such as rigid territorial rights, undue dominance of race, group and party, wrong stress on social status and the like. Only compliance with intuitive instead of instinctive guidance, can correct and realign the course of mankind. It is time for Immanent God to be enabled to throw off the shackles which we, whether through ignorance or perversity, insist on keeping tightly bound.

Our civilization is rapidly nearing the point of no-return. If it persists in continuing along its present extension of the Natural Phase, it can only find a horror of frustration and suffering in a hell deeper and hotter than any yet known. This is a time for self-choice by mankind as a whole. It has been warned, it must choose, and each individual must help. There is still more of the ape in man than he knows, and it must be realized and eradicated. He must ween himself from the ways of the ape before ever he can find the divine status to which he is heir. The future hinges on the individual, for true conviction can come only individually, and this includes each one of us. Those who read and digest this book intelligently cannot avoid the issue. They can put it aside, they can bury it in the memory clutter of inconsequentials, but again and again the thought of it will return to those who are approaching ripeness, to all who have achieved the necessary level of consciousness. And if it makes them uneasy or uncomfortable it is doing its work. If, in some cases, it succeeds in making individuals happy, then it will have done its work.

The Inward Search

Bearing in mind The Focus, and the expansion of it in the Commentary, it will be fairly obvious what we need to do to find God and Truth, for these are one. We have to remember only, that the spiritual entity which is our core, inner being or real self, is a unit of God, and the way becomes obvious. It is the inner or inward search. This search is not anything new. Men have been making it for thousands of years. After all, if we have intuitional guidance, that is, the voice of conscience developed until it guides all our actions and if this guidance is of The Creator, we can only look for it in The Creator, and where does the voice of conscience come from, inside or outside? It comes from within because it is the inherent reaction of the spiritual entities which are our real selves. Instinct in animals is the parallel inherent reaction to the spiritual entities, but the guidance is physical, whereas intuition in man is concerned with spiritual guidance.

Man today does not heed the intuitive voice in him, partly because it is weak due to the thought barrier between himself and it, a barrier which he has created. He is the only animal with free choice, and can therefore cut free from natural guidance, and unlike other animals which have no reasoning faculty, and therefore no thought of doing anything else than follow instinct, (unless taught), he can cut adrift from it and follow his own path. To regain in strength the natural guidance which in most people is now weak, and in some almost lost, the only way then, is to break back through the thought barrier which is damping down, or even almost entirely smothering the intuitive voice. Do not let confusion arise in thinking that there is a duality of entity in an individual. There is not. The only duality is that of outlook by the one entity, the one being material through the physical senses and thought, and the other spiritual through what we are calling intuition, which is inherent knowledge of the Mind Image, and of the ever present guidance towards it. Concentration on both these outlooks cannot be made at the same time, and one must be stopped in order to find the other. Man today has so neglected to use intuition, that in most of us it is but a faint shadow of what it can and should be, and in many it is almost nonexistent, that is. almost completely unheard, for it can never cease to exist. Most individuals today therefore, conduct their lives almost completely from a personal angle, and as there is no other co-ordinator of personal angles, individual desires clash with consequent pain and suffering. So it will always be while personality in the individual ranges from that just clear of the beast, to that just short of God.

The only way in which alignment can be obtained, is by foregoing the personal angle and turning to the alternative, the other outlook available to the inner entity, that is the intuitive one. To obtain this it is necessary to stop the sensory physical outlook first. This means that sense impressions must be prevented from impinging on the consciousness. The body must first be in a restful position although not lying down. Sitting or kneeling in an easy posture with the trunk upright, and as nearly as possible completely relaxed. Everyone knows that, at times, one falls into a condition of reverie when, though apparently looking at an object, one is looking as we say, through it. In other words it is not allowed to be consciously recognized. This condition for the senses, mainly sight and hearing, must be aimed at. It helps to close the eyes at first. Do not make a mistake here. The darkness required is not just that found by looking at the inside of closed eyelids. This is only a relative state and is useless and must be removed from the consciousness. The inner darkness which is necessary comes rather as if the eyeballs withdrew and swivelled and looked inwards into absolute blackness. This must be found. Difficult at the start, it gradually gets easier, and one reaches a stage when attention has been completely withdrawn from all external sights, sounds, etc.

Next comes the question of thought control. With the body relaxed, a continuous thought sequence on a pre-chosen subject must be concentrated upon, all irrelevant thoughts being dismissed before they enter this conscious sequence. Concentration should be continued to a pin point. After a while it becomes easy to do this, and then, after intense concentration, it should suddenly be given up and a completely no-thought condition found. This should be maintained as long as possible, all the fleeting, flickering, darting, irrelevant thoughts which attempt to enter the consciousness, being prevented from doing so. Perseverance with this will gradually permit of the condition being obtained at will almost immediately, as it were at the snap of a switch. Sleep must be guarded against, for the relaxation of body and mind can easily result in slipping into sleep instead of maintaining alertness. Incidentally, this technique need not necessarily involve one in a belief in God, and can be followed at least to the stage of pin-point concentration without such belief, and yet with much benefit to the individual, both in relaxation and in the solving of personal problems. This is the first stage, and for many will take much time and patience. Although habit of any sort is dangerous, even good habit, the best way for the majority is probably a set time each day with this, once started, rigorously adhered to. At first, for many, it will seem almost hopeless, and much perseverance will be necessary. It is a matter for the individual. If it is urgent enough for him he will do it.

When it is found possible to come easily to this stage of blankness of mind, that is a condition of no thought whatsoever, the next step may be tried. This is to prepare a thought sequence and, completely relaxed, continue the line of reasoning to the absolute limit of the individual intellectual capacity, then suddenly switch to the no-thought condition and maintain it, quite relaxed but mentally extremely alert, almost prayerfully alert, for the slightest sense of an answer. How the answer comes cannot be explained. Seen? Heard? Felt? All that can be said is that it seeps into the consciousness so softly as to be almost apologetic. It may be a long time before success is achieved, but as surely as one humbly believes in an intelligence greater than the individual human intelligence, and as one is quietly persistent, sooner or later an answer will come. Not always as expected, but even when unexpected always worthy of following up intellectually, and then resubmitting later.

Up to this point the investigation has been on a psychic level, and results will correspond to the level on which it is conducted. Many reaching this stage may be content to stop, happy in the increased concentration which helps in the daily problems, particularly when inspirational answers are obtained, and also in the now easily found relaxation of mind in the stopping, for short periods, of all thought. Some however, having succeeded thus far, and encouraged by results are now prepared to carry belief beyond the intellect only, may wish to proceed to the next stage. This stage however cannot be undertaken successfully by anyone who is not willing to admit in all sincerity, that there exists something greater than the human intellect, not this time however just of an intellectual order, but some power which is responsible for us in all respects. Something which made us, guides us, and sets a code of conduct for us. A power of which we are a part and to which, sometime, we must return. A belief in a continuity of life and experience before and after this life. If, then, the individual concerned finds himself able to acknowledge in humility and sincerity that there is this something greater than he, he proceeds as follows. Start with concentration on a chosen thought sequence again, but this time let the subject be of a spiritual nature. The best, and here can only be repeated what has been said for centuries, are those of self-enquiry such as 'Who am I?', 'What am I?', 'Who is this speaking?' 'What made me do that?' etc. The sequence should follow a logical course in eliminating this, and that, and it should continue until intensely concentrated, and to the absolute intellectual limit. Then, in faith in that which is greater than the one enquiring, and greater than the human intellect, the question should be dropped, in desperation, into the silence of the void. Note that the stage of desperation is necessary, for nothing short of it will produce what is wanted. Having gently pushed the question out, wait absolutely still but very alert, not allowing a single thought to enter the consciousness. The wait may be long. It may fail and the whole procedure have to be tried again, and sometimes again and again and again. But sooner or later an answer will come. After that first one, answers will come more readily, and real progress will be made. It will be seen that the belief in something greater than the individual is necessary, because the last move in this stage is one of pure faith. Faith in something greater than the intellect. This will come hardly to some, but if previous results have been good, then faith will gradually have built up over a period, and the last step will not be so great as might be imagined. If this all sounds terrifically complicated do not be deterred, for it works itself out as you go along.

When the search has reached this advanced stage, and you are trying to find out who or what you are, or why you are here, etc. don't start searching inside for Jesus the Christ, or Gautama the Buddha, or Krishna, or anyone else to act as an intermediary. There is no need to think of, or appeal to, any intermediary, for contact between a man and his God is direct. After you have identified yourself completely, then you will find, and come to understand better, the intermediaries of the various religions. The reading of all this in a book, or the hearing of it verbally, will not make any difference to the experienced conviction. Words will only guide to the conviction, but above all else keep a completely open mind, and do not allow any preconceived ideas to influence you in any way. Don't forget that man does not need to wait for God to give him anything. If a man will prepare himself properly, he can himself initiate the search, and he is heir to what he can find. A man can only understand that which he is, and there is nothing he is not. If you seek diligently enough, and ask perseveringly enough, there is nothing you cannot find or know.

Results of the search depend upon the condition of the one making it. If you do not get results, you need to find out what is wrong in you, correct it and try again. It's no use asking anyone else. Only you yourself can know what is wrong, and only you yourself can correct it. First the individual has to be capable of sufficient bodily control to bring about a completely relaxed bodily condition. This is not easy but it can be done. Then he must control the mind until it is completely relaxed and blank. No-one however, can expect to get advanced intellectual answers, unless he has a good grasp of the particular subject and can put the question with the necessary pin-pointed concentration. The answers come as and when you are genuinely and distressfully perplexed. They do not short circuit hard labour. They do give inspirational results, which would not normally have been reached with any amount of hard labour.

If the search is of a spiritual nature, then preparation must include decent thinking and action, and general clean living, with gradual conscious control of all bad habits, and of all actions done for personal gratification of the senses. A gradual ascendency of mind over body and emotions is essential.

In short, good results generally are commensurate with preparation. The greatest factor in producing them is humility.

A Scientific Approach to God

During the last forty years or so, I have pursued what I believe to be a reasonably critical attitude towards the approach to God, and I stand by the results obtained. I date this approach back to the day when I turned my back on the Christian religion as it is presented. It has taken a long time, but I believe only because, at first, it was not consciously followed with the particular end in view, and it has been only of later years that the real end has been recognized. If the latter had been stated in the beginning, and there had been the experience such as has been mine to guide me, I believe that I might have attained the same end in, possibly, half the time : perhaps less. This however applies only if development of the one commencing the approach is ripe enough for the purpose. Given that, and there must be a good many such, then I believe that a reasonably scientific approach can be made, and followed through to the end I have found.

From what has been said elsewhere in the book, it should not be inferred that a particularly high intellectual level is essential. The will to succeed, to press forward regardless of everything, is important. A great love of mankind is not necessary in the beginning as it grows gradually with understanding. Love for each and every man and woman may never be achieved, unless the willingness to serve each one as normal procedure, is regarded as love. But the love of mankind must, and will, increase as time passes.

This method is impossible of further proof by myself. It may be however, that there are some in whom the question is so urgent that they will be prepared to devote many years to confirmation for themselves. Devote is the right word, for anything short of devotion to the task will not be sufficient.

There are a number of paths which must be followed—not necessarily all at the same time, but not all separately. They will mingle fairly well after a first period of experiment and adjustment. The same level will not however, be attained on all these paths. Some individuals are more suited at the start to some paths than to others, and their ways will necessarily vary. If the level attained fairly quickly on one path becomes comparatively high, then probably the level on another, or others, may be comparatively low. But everyone should go some way along most of the paths.

As one requisite is complete relaxation of the physical body, a fair conscious control of the muscles is required so that, at will, one may find physical relaxation in a moment. Watch a dog lying down to rest. It slumps into complete relaxation and can be asleep in a matter of seconds. Then if you test one of its front paws it will move at a touch as if on a well oiled hinge. This is complete limpness, and the sort of relaxation to aim at. When you do this in bed, you actually feel the different parts of yourself, including the head, sinking into the bedding. The best time, at first, is when lying in bed ready for sleep. Lie on the back with arms by the sides, and concentrate on first one and then another part, relaxing the muscles of each when concentrated on in turn. With perseverance you will feel the parts becoming heavy, so that they sink into the bedding. Continue this until you are able to relax all of them together. Then it will be found that the same can be done in different positions, as when lying on your side, and eventually when sitting or kneeling. A slowing down of the breathing rate will also assist.

Breath control also should be included, the aim being to deepen the breathing gradually and so to slow it down. Exercises will soon help in this respect. Eventually it will be found that when the body is completely relaxed and the breathing deep, the breath rate will be slowed considerably. This helps one to get to sleep and also to acquire emotional control.

Relaxation of the mind follows and eventually the complete stopping of all thought. This has been dealt with already, under the title 'The Inward Search', so we will pass on, with just the reminder that the purpose here is to achieve a complete blankness of mind with, not unconsciousness, but on the contrary extreme alertness.

Emotional control must be achieved, and to many, perhaps to the majority, this may be the most difficult task of all. It must be done however, for the whole Truth can never be realized through the emotional approach. Emotions are of the physical sphere and always have an object, whereas the sincere and honest approach to the finding of Truth can only be found with a mind completely open, and free from all preconceived ideas. So an emotional approach is out of the question, and will spoil any intellectual approach that may be attempted. A figurative foot therefore, should be kept ready to stamp, at will, on the emotions, so that an ice-cold intellectual approach can be made when required. Do not let there be any mistake here. This does not mean that one becomes completely unemotional and inhuman. Like all else in these procedures, it is the control at will which is aimed at, and without which nothing real can be achieved. But, when the control is not necessary, emotion will take its normal place in the every-day individual life, although never in the uncontrolled way which governs the life and belief of many. It is a very severe task for it will be found, at times, to affect relationships with wife, children, parents, relatives and friends, who will probably never understand what one is doing, even when it is possible to take them into one's confidence.

It takes considerable courage to face directly, and without flinching, the consequences of a non-deviating approach. Don't treat this lightly, for the chances of misunderstanding are great. Everyone at times will misunderstand one's motives. It can be, and at times must be, a lonely road. Others cannot be told of it, at least in the later stages. One has to become, temporarily at least, a solitary.

There is service to others: help in many and various ways. It should be personal service whenever possible, and it should include, not only help to those in good health, but also to the sick and dying. If necessary, or felt desirable, a period as a male or female probationer nurse will help. There should be experience of the human being in all its aspects, including its smelliness and filth, its disease and death. The limited experience gained in voluntary first aid work or nursing, especially in hospitals, is

91

valuable, and may be sufficient to the purpose. On the other hand sometimes the experience will come in the home. And if one is not prepared to do this, even to the extent at times of having to turn away to vomit, then one is not yet fit to go on.

Habits have to be faced, and any which cause others distress to be stopped. Those indulged in for the gratification of the physical senses, though not necessarily all of them, should be either stopped or controlled. Once controlled, some can then be indulged in moderation. It is primarily the control which is important, and the main object is to dissociate oneself from the rulings of the physical senses. Man must control the physical body and senses, not the reverse. Sexual intercourse should cease for a longish period as one approaches the climax of effort, and this should be while the desire for it is still strong, not when one is old and the desire burned out, or almost so, of its own accord. This does not mean that it need be stopped permanently. Once the stranglehold of the desires has been broken, and true enlightenment found, then if still desired, sexual intercourse, always in moderation, can be resumed, but this time without it being in any way a ruling passion, or obtruding in other aspects of life. Fasting in moderation is good. Please note that word moderation, for to go to extremes can do more harm than good to one's health. It may also end in one becoming obsessed with method, thus mistaking it for the end.

All these ways, or as many as are followed, (and the more the better), are not distinct and separate, although they may seem to be at times. They all play a part in the overall pattern of preparation for the climax. Gradually will come, if not already present, the necessity of honourable conduct, including the telling of the truth as known at all times. This in itself can make one very unpopular, but that cannot be helped. All lies should be avoided. In general, the voice of conscience will be heard clearer, and more often, and should be heeded.

It is essential that one should not become obsessed by all this procedure, and one or two active pastimes such as walking, golf, tennis and gardening will help, not only to preserve a balance, but also to keep one physically fit and as closely as possible in touch with nature. Gradually as time goes on, it will be found that superficialities begin first to bore one, and then to irritate. They will be eschewed, and one will slowly come to live a simpler life, finding much more satisfaction in simpler things.

This may sound terribly complicated, and as if one's whole time might be required over many years. It is not so, for much of it dovetails together fairly easily, and after a few years it begins to develop naturally. All this leads gradually to a humility which is essential to the final end. And remember that all one does, all the help one may give, must be with detachment. That is, without consideration of any repercussions on oneself. Do what you know to be right for you in your particular circumstances, and take no thought for the morrow.

I firmly believe that many living today can, by this method, achieve in this life the enlightenment which must come to every-one sometime. It is the speeding, the intended conscious speed-ing, of an intended natural process in man. A coming into line with the laws laid down in the beginning to guide man back to his spiritual home. But like can merge only with like. And before men can remerge with God, he must become as God, or The One, or Brahman, or whatever one may call it. The One is perhaps the easiest term in all contexts. And many in this life time can approach very closely to the spiritual man of The Image, The Son of God.

This is a method of investigation for the individual, a method for the integration of personal experience through meditation, and I suggest that it is a scientific method, and may be proven by many individuals for themselves. Not every individual, but then not every one can conduct a scientific enquiry. But an individual with the sufficient urge to make himself able to understand spiritual laws, is in the same position as he who has the urge to understand physical laws, and is willing to work many years in learning how to do so.

The impression may have been given that such a routine over a number of years must result in an over-serious outlook, in fact possibly in a rather miserable sort of life. Strangely enough (or is it?) just the reverse has happened to the writer. Although neither he nor his wife are blessed, at this stage of life, with very good physical health, it is doubtful if ever half-an-hour passes without them laughing together. It was not always so.

Interim

You dare to talk to me of fantasy?
I who have seen beyond the mortal eye
That looks but on the shadow of the Real?
You dare to pit your arguments against
That which has come with such authority
From where the reason must itself appeal?
With flowing thought from dark and silent skies,
That lifts a man as far as he may rise
Until no heaven and earth are left, for here
In The Original all disappear;
And there remains but that so bright and clear
As is The Eternal, infinitely wise.

Interim

About two and a half years of work passed in sorting out the hundreds of separate communications of the revelation, and discarding all but the ones which are certainly not personal to myself, and then in rearranging the comparatively few left into a reasonable sequence. Then came the task of relating what remained to current belief, and I have been busy on that now for about another three years. During this third period (allowing approximately $1\frac{1}{2}$ years of revelation as the first), there has been great excitement in me at times, when I found the parts of various existing religious beliefs combining fairly easily into a reasonable and satisfying whole, and also when scientific findings fitted in with a click. It was rather like shaking up together seven or eight huge jig-saw puzzles and then, out of the pile, finding that some of each would fit together to form a picture which was not one of those shown on the original boxes. The clue to the operation was the picture given by The Focus.

If anyone thinks that I sat down at a table with piles of books, notepaper and pencils, and coldly and solemnly tabulated all the religious, philosophical, metaphysical and scientific points involved, and then worked out a completely reasonable amalgam incorporating all of them, then that one is quite mad—just as I would have been before I had finished. It was, quite literally, by the reverse process of the stoppage of all thought that this came to be. If you consider that I am mad because I am able, at will, to stop all thought, and now after years at it, do so for long periods, well and good, but at least there have been others besides me who were able to do it and, for all I know, there are others doing it now. Any of you, if you fulfil the necessary conditions can prove it for yourselves, and remember that for this part only of the process, that is the stopping of all thought at will, you do not need to have any religious belief, or even to be in search of one. And if that is not bringing, at least the beginning of this, into the scientific field, then I do not know what will.

To come to the fitting in of the parts. I started with The Focus and with Christianity. It soon became obvious that the fitting in could be accomplished, but that a good deal of reinterpretation was necessary. In the light of The Focus therefore, I started on this task and found that it was possible to interpret quite a lot of the Christian scriptures in a different way from that accepted by the Christian Church. In doing this I discovered that basically, much of the accepted interpretation would fit in, if the accent were altered. In fact Christian belief came to look, to me, like a badly phrased song, which not only does not make sense but which irritates the sensitive listener. For example, I found that I could agree with 'The Fall', if it were in a different setting, and the same with the idea of self-choice, and so on. So a certain amount of the evidence from which Christian belief is formulated fitted into The Focus. A similar process applied to other religions gave a similar result, and The Focus was then revealed as being an amalgam of parts of each of the religions, plus the parts of this new revelation which are not included in any of them. And these new parts seem to be in relation to the present existing religions, as humus is to the mineral parts of soil. It binds all the separate parts into a coherent whole.

Despite the cleansing, or mind-purging, or whatever else you care to call it which I have experienced, it may be that I am still biased. You will each decide for yourselves. I believe that this new belief is nearer to Truth than any other yet on record. In other words I believe that each of the existing great religions has a part of the truth, but that no one of them has the whole, also that further revelation from time to time will provide still more. It is therefore only by taking the partial truths of each of them, and combining these into a coherent whole, that we shall ever approach a totality of truth.

Before proceeding to the next section of the book, which is Christianity in Focus, let stress be laid on the supreme and paramount importance of approaching the matter with an open mind. This request is addressed in particular to those of the Christian faith who may be reading this, because their beliefs are set so hard in many cases, that a sledge hammer rather than nut crackers is required to break them down. So if the mind is not prepared for big breaks with tradition, put the book away now, and forget you ever opened it.

At the risk of reiteration, a few more words on the nature of revelation must be added. Dismiss the idea that prophecy or revelation is in the direct words of a transcendent god, which come streaming with great authority to the chosen channel of prophet, seer or sage, often accompanied by the sounding of brass, or the visions of angels, etc. All these things may be experienced, but they are the fantasies of immature spirituality.

Can you imagine what it means to have the mind suddenly able to reach to the storehouse of the knowledge and wisdom of all times? Suddenly to be freed from the shackles of the flesh and the physical senses? Suddenly to soar through infinite space, through the colours of a million rainbows, and the throbbing of a million melodies? Suddenly to be able to stand on the top of a mountain, and proclaim to the whole world that all truth is here for the taking? When you have done this, you will have experienced the fantasy of the prophet, due to the suddenly released and freed spirit.

When this first taste of freedom is over, and one returns to the heaviness of the flesh, the words and pictures will be eagerly re-called. And if, in the simple faith of superstition, they are believed to be the words of a transcendent god to mankind, then they will be recorded and received as such. And so, if permitted, they will remain until some-day, when developed intellectual perception has removed more of the scales of superstition, someone else has a similar experience. It is then realized that the initial revelation, with all the accompanying fantasy, is mainly a revelation personal to the recipient, and is so designed in various extreme forms as to remove the bias and prejudices of the particular mind concerned. It is, in other words, a purging of an individual mind to enable it to receive, with the least possible distortion, the general revelation to follow. And it is man himself, suddenly identified as Son of God, or in other words Immanent God, who produces this personal revelation, and purges the earthbound mind of the previous ego or little self. It has been looking through two windows, one only dimly. Suddenly the dim one shows a blaze of light, and as this strengthens, it gradually overwhelms the light from the other window, but not until this process is completed is the blaze of the light in the second window pierced, and the real picture behind it is seen undistorted. The general revelation which follows is consciously instigated by man, (in his new capacity), and is the deliberate delvings of a cleansed mind, into the Real which lies close behind earthly illusion. As time goes on the tentative methods of question and answer fade away, because one becomes, not exterior to the Real or Truth, but a part of it. Never, while in the body is this truth completely free from distortion, but it becomes relatively so as one proceeds.

And the old-time prophecies are partly good, for although they are the outlook of a cleansed mind, they also include much of the fantasy which was of the personal cleansing, and is not only confusing to others, but can even be dangerous, if they relate it literally to themselves.

So, as stated before, all original revelation needs re-interpreting, if possible by the original recipient when more spiritually mature. Failing this it should be always suspect, and used only in the light of reason, for a man partially blinded by fantasy cannot clearly see reality.

There is still very much to be done, and years of work lie ahead, but at least something coherent has developed, and so can be used as a framework on which may be hung further particulars as they are seen.

The writer is not a scholar as will probably be obvious. He does not regret this, for he believes that if he had been a scholar of any standing, his scholarship might have blinded him to the understanding which has become so obvious, and is now his. Neither is there any apology in the statement, for if the book is not of usual conformation, and if perhaps there is some reiteration, these are small things for which no shame is felt. The statement then is made because the author has been at the mercy of a family Bible, a number of cheap paper-backed editions of various works, and books from a small branch library—all in

100

English. In this book therefore is offered what is believed to be the spirit of the evidence at disposal, rather than compliance with the letter. The writer does believe however, that it will not be difficult to smooth out whatever discrepancies there may be due to his lack of scholarship.

Christianity
in
Focus

'I say unto you, Though he will not rise and give him because he is his friend, yet because of his importunity he will rise and give him as many as he needeth.

'And I say unto you, Ask, and it shall be given you; seek, and ye shall find; knock, and it shall be opened unto you.'

(Luke xi, 8 and 9)

The Bible:
Creation and the Fall

Let us consider again the account of the Creation as relating to man, and as given in *Genesis*. There is a double account of it, the first being chapter one and the first three verses of chapter two, the second account following on from there. It is generally believed that this is a duplication, and also that it is almost certain that the accounts were written by two different men or groups.

Now in the light of 'The Focus', let us reread and reconsider the whole account of the Creation. It will be seen that it is not duplication, but describes two separate happenings. We see that the first account is intended to convey the Mind Image, and the second the actual physical creation. The first which is very short deals with the forming of the Image, from something without form, into a complete image with a path planned to it, the culmination of the path being the creature known as Man. In the second account, God made the earth habitable by mist from the earth, which watered the whole face of the ground. Then He made man, vegetation, animals and birds etc. In this extremely short statement, is included the evolution of the whole of the Natural Phase, up to the emergence of man from the ranks of the higher animals. His asking man to name the other creatures, is a sign that man is superior to all else in the physical world.

The two accounts differ in one very important particular. In the first, dealing with the creation of the mind image, this occurs, 'And God said, let us make man in our image, after our likeness, and let them have dominion over the fish of the sea, the fowl of the air, and over the cattle, and over all the earth, and over every creeping thing that creepeth upon the earth. So God created man in his own image, in the image of God created He them.'

On the seventh day he rested.

Then starts the second account. This concentrates on man, for man, the crux of the whole Plan and Image, was of first importance in the actual creation, which is seen as the evolution of the whole Natural Phase up to the emergence of Man.

The Image had to be complete before the beginning of actual physical creation, for into every part and particle of actual creation, had to go the unit of intelligence of God with the inherent knowledge of the Image. Only in this way could come guidance through the Natural Phase up to the Image. For from the beginning this evolutionary period was for the purpose of providing a vehicle for the spiritual entity, which from then on had to have continuous existence and development, in order to fulfil the original purpose of God in 'It revealing Itself to Itself'.

So, at the beginning of the second account we have, in Chapter ii, Verse 4, 'These are the generations of the heavens and of the earth, when they were created, in the day that the Lord God made the earth and the heavens.' Here begins the actual physical creation of the earth and the heavens. This does not necessarily refer only to the earth, but probably to the whole universe with its many bodies, and is no more intended to be taken literally, than the seventh day as being the length of one of our days. The next verse makes it clear that the earth so formed, is not yet ready for the plants and herbs which are to be the next step for it says, 'And every plant of the field before it was in the earth, and every herb of the field before it grew : For the Lord God had not caused it to rain upon the earth, and there was not a man to till the ground'. Then continuing, verse 6 says, 'But there went up a mist from the earth, and watered the whole face of the ground'. There we have the whole of millions of years of evolution from the first swirling of gas in the Void, to the stage when the vapour from the cooling earth condensed, and fell back as rain, to bring about conditions suitable for vegetable and animal life, for everything is in the Void, all that ever was or will be, and all that is necessary for an emergence, is to make suitable conditions. Then follows the forming of man, animal and vegetable life, but with the accent always on Man, the Transition Link, the crux of the Image, The Word of the Image become the flesh in physical creation.

So, when He had completed the mind image and formulated

the Plan, He rested, and then began the actual physical creation. We now come to man. This time there is an actual physical earth in being, and so 'The Lord God formed man of the dust of the ground'.

You have noticed the difference? In the first account, 'Let us make man in our image, after our likeness'. That is He made man in His image. And in that image He made him in His likeness. Not only that but it is repeated later. 'So God created man in His own image, in the image of God created He him'. That is, He created man in His own likeness, in His mind image. Not yet from the dust of the ground, for there was as yet no actual earth from which to make dust. This was reserved for the second account, that of the actual physical creation. Also note that here no mention is made of the image, for its creation had been completed before the seventh day on which He rested.

Another difference between the two accounts is also worthy of note. In the first one dealing with The Mind Image, it says several times that, 'And God saw that it was good'. On the last occasion in verse 31, after all was completed, it is even more emphatic and says, 'And God saw everything that he had made, and, behold, it was very good'. So that the Image was made in perfection.

In the second account there is not a single mention of His satisfaction, for the creation now is the actual physical creation or evolution, and man, emerging from the animal kingdom, is still little more than a brute. So, at the creation of man, that is at his emergence as a living soul, all is very far from the perfection of the image.

And here is 'The Fall'. It is the fall from the perfection of the Mind Image to the raw state of the physical creation.

At this point in the emergent creation then, God breathed into the nostrils of man the breath of life, and man became a living soul. That is, at this stage God gave to man the faculty of reason, the use of which would enable man to free himself from the strict guidance and control of the Natural Phase, and become an independent individual entity. This is the point of climax of the Natural Phase, which was designed to evolve this species of physical body, capable of being used by the inhabiting spiritual entity to cut free from the Natural Phase. Thus it could commence an independent existence in a new phase, which will be called the Psychic Phase. From this point onwards the Natural Phase, as a means of evolution of the physical body of man, becomes less important, for it has served its main purpose. Although its dictates are not now the paramount guiding force, yet it still must be worked with, for man cannot alter its course and must always, while in the physical body, be affected by it. God Himself would not alter its course for, having started it rolling, it must roll to its end, which may be a multiple one, not confined to this planet and man. So the man made from the dust of the ground was physical man, and in him the inner spiritual entity which is in all creatures, became an independent entity, being awakened to the possibility by the faculty of reason endowed at this stage, and which divided man from all other animals.

Emerging man had no spiritual life before his psychic quality developed and it was the evolutionary stage of thought development to the point of reasoning which started it. Symbolically, in the Bible, God breathed into his nostrils 'the breath of life'. This had nothing to do with the air or breath which is necessary to maintain life in the physical body, and which had kept alive animal life, including man's predecessors, for millions of years. This breath particularly mentioned was something special to the species man as he emerged from the ruck. It was the spiritual breath of life or faculty of reason which made him 'a living soul', an entity capable of continuous individual spiritual development. He was the only one of the animal species thus endowed just as, in the Biblical account, only man received this gift. Confusion arises because, of necessity, the account in the Bible compresses millions of years of development into a few words. For instance— 'And the Lord God formed man of the dust of the ground, and breathed into his nostrils the breath of life. . .'. These two statements read as if the actions were more or less simultaneous, whereas millions of years intervened between the appearance of the first animal in the chain of species ending in man, and the bestowal (or development?) of the special 'breath of life'. Just as, in the account of animals generally, the Bible says—'And out of the ground the Lord God formed every beast of the field and every fowl of the air, and brought them unto Adam to see what he would call them. . .'. Again the long interval between the two happenings, for these other creatures were made millions of years before the first Adam emerged to name them.

Now, therefore, man was capable of choosing his own way. The way out from the beginning up to this stage had been guided by instinctive group behaviour, progressive with the increasing complexity of evolution, and not dependent upon the thoughtful decision of the individual. Now, however, man was enabled to make thoughtful and reasoned decisions, contrary to the instinctive drive. He therefore became subject to error, for his progress was seen only from his own individual and very limited viewpoint. Moreover as men increased in number and, wandering apart from each other had different varieties of experience, so viewpoints became different, and those on progress less uniform. So at this stage it was necessary that guidance should be given, to replace the fading instinctive guidance of the Natural Phase. This, in the symbolism of the Bible, was given by eating of the tree of life or, in other words, intuitive spiritual guidance, which became gradually apparent to man as he developed, mainly through the channel known as conscience. By means of this intuition man was enabled, if he wished, to react immediately to its guidance without any intermediate thought process, just as in his past experience he had reacted to instinct. It was necessary, however, that there should be a difference between the applications of the two behaviours, for the instinctive way out through the material had been compulsive whereas, if the self-revelation of It was to be accomplished, then man, a spiritual entity, had to be severed completely from the compulsion of the Plan, to return freely of his own individual choice when he wished. The return by the intuitive spiritual way therefore, could not be one of compulsion. The guidance had to be constantly available, but taken only by free choice of the individual. This, again in the symbolism of the Bible, was shown through the tree of the knowledge of good and evil, as opposed to the tree of life. God warned man that he should not eat of the tree of the knowledge of good and evil, and that if he did so he would surely die. Here then came the choice for man. If he accepted the offered intuitional guidance by eating of the tree of life, then he would not know death, but would have everlasting life. If, however, he chose to ignore that guidance, and to eat of the tree of the knowledge of good and evil, then he would die. Action in accordance with natural divinely intended law, either instinct or intuition, is immediate without any free choice of the individual concerned or, in the case of intuition, with relinquished free choice. Therefore action permitted by this free choice, which is against the dictates of intuitive guidance is error and, once this is realized, if the error is persisted in it becomes sin. Purely intuitive action, therefore, carries with it no spiritual consequences. Error in ignorance may have no consequences but brings warnings by way of conscience, or through the hurts done by a man to another. Having himself been hurt by an action, this is his warning. If then a man in his turn does the same action to another, it is with the conscious knowledge that he is doing harm and consequences will be incurred. Revelations from time to time also bring warnings.

Referring back to the free choice given to man, the one way he may go is the direct intuitive one back to the original. Had he been able to take this way, and sever all connection with the instinctive way in the very early stages of his independent existence, there would have been none of the evil which has dogged him since his emergence. But he could not cut adrift quickly from the Natural Phase and so, at this stage, had no real free choice. This came at a much later stage in his development. Theoretically it was there all the time, but practically, it was not intended that he should find it in the early stages. As pointed out in the Commentary under the title Evil, he must continue as an independent entity for a while, else his whole purpose in becoming such is lost.

Genesis, chapter iii, verses 22, 23, and 24, may be seen as confirmation. With the usual symbolism, man has chosen the way by the tree of the knowledge of Good and Evil. God will not allow him the chance of changing his mind, and denies him immediate access to the Tree of Life (the intuitive way), and places guards between it and him which, symbolically, stand for the thought barrier or body which was spoken of previously. The flaming sword which turns every way is the restless, darting, never-ceasing thoughts which continually fill the mind, so that access to intuition is impossible, until the way is found to still the thoughts. Man is turned out of the garden to till the ground. In other words, to work out his own solution to the problem of regaining access to the Tree of Life. Or, if you prefer it, to work out his own salvation.*

* See also under The Bible—Free Choice, p. 121.

The Bible:
Adam, Eve, The Garden and The Serpent

The sexual act in the male is a compulsive urge. It had to be so, when the preservation of the species was a main essential of the way out to The Image. And this is so in man in particular for, a species sufficient to the purpose in view had evolved and it was essential that it should survive against all others. So, particularly in man, the compulsive urge had to be.

It also had to be that man should have dominion over woman, and this for the same reason. That God intended this is shown symbolically in *Genesis*, chapter ii, verses 19 and 20. Here God is making the beasts and fowls and bringing them to Adam, that is to man, for him to name, thus signifying that he has dominion over them, and thus implementing the promise of the Mind Image as in *Genesis* i, verse 26. Then, in chapter ii, verses 22 and 23, God makes woman and, as also in the case of the beasts and the fowl, brings her to Adam and Adam names her, thus indicating that man has dominion over her also, (which dominion could be relaxed in the future as reason dictated, and by mutual understanding and agreement). There are two differences however. Firstly, woman is made as a help meet for man. Secondly, she is made, symbolically, from a part of the body of Adam, that is a rib, and not from the dust of the ground, as were Adam and the beasts etc. In its previous evolutionary progress before emergence as man, the species had male and female members, so that this making of a help meet for Adam, was not indicative of the making of a female for the male, but really literally as it says, as a help meet in his journey onwards. And his journey onwards from the stage of the emergent man, was to be a return to the original spiritual state, and this can only be accomplished by rising above the physical state, breaking down the bonds of the physical body and sensory hold, with its sensual satisfactions. In this then, was woman to be the help meet of man.

112

Recent scientific findings tell us that the female of the species nearest to man and arising from a common stock, that is of the monkeys and apes, already uses her sex in ways other than purely sexual. She tempts the male to copulate merely as a form of social submission, or in order to appease him. Woman, then, starting at this stage, and with the faculty of reason soon showing her that she could use her sex to gain power over the male, did just this, and in doing so acted directly against her purpose as help meet. Thus it was that she ate of the fruit of the tree of the knowledge of good and evil, and gave it also to her husband, and he ate with her. And so it was that the little personal self, which lusts for power and for the gratification of the physical senses, raised its head, and this little personal self is the Serpent of *Genesis*. And man and woman, when they realized what they were doing in setting up their own objects and ends in opposition to the true way and end, were ashamed.

The second difference in the making of woman must now be considered. The foregoing has been dealt with from the standpoint of woman, and it follows that woman acts wrongly in sexually tempting man for personal ends. But it may be said that this does not also indict man, for the act in him being originally a compulsive urge, he is not to be blamed for accepting the temptation at the invitation of woman. Let us consider then, the reason for his shame. *Genesis* chapter ii, verses 21, 22, 23, 24, are symbolic of the fact that man and woman were intended to be one in their journey to their intended spiritual end of overcoming the flesh. (This does not mean that the same pair go through all earthly lives together.) Thus man yearns for woman because being made, symbolically, out of his rib she is part of him, bone of his bone and flesh of his flesh, and, as Adam said, a man shall leave all else to cleave to her. And, he said, the two shall be one flesh. And in this meeting of the two in the flesh, the man knows if the union is mutual yearning of the one for the other, for when a man and a woman are truly in love, and the sexual act is undertaken only at the behest of love on both sides, neither can be mistaken in the attitude of the other. And man knows when the woman's attitude is not purely of love and, if he indulges then, it is in the knowledge that he returns to the animal compulsive urge, and gives precedence to the flesh over the spirit. And so there is the blame also in him, as well as in the woman. And God said that the little personal self should crawl in shame all the days of its life. And woman should come to hate the sexual act of the animal personal self, and resent it. And the personal self should feel remorse. For to the sensual animal self of man, the sexual act is an end in itself and this is what the woman resents, for a woman reacts rather to the man or to motherhood than to the act itself.

To the woman He said (*Genesis* chapter iii, verse 16), that He would greatly multiply her sorrow and her conception. And it is so. Turning once more to the animals nearest to man, the monkeys and the apes, and to the findings of science, we see that only copulation during a heat period will result in conception and the production of offspring, whilst copulation out of heat periods is free from such consequences. Thus, in changing this in the human female, God has greatly multiplied her chances of conception, from what it might have been, for the periods of freedom from consequences in childbirth are short, and in any case not infallible. So she has not sufficiently long safe periods, to enable her to satisfy the compulsive urge of the male by natural means without the consequence of childbirth, as she would have had, if allowed to combine the ability of conscious regulation in agreement between human male and female, with the longer safe periods of the animal. And so, not only her conception but her sorrow also, is greatly increased as promised. Her sorrow is increased also because, as *Genesis* chapter iii, verse 16, says, a woman's desire shall be to her husband, in other words she shall have a craving for a husband and for motherhood, despite the suffering it brings her.

And He said to the little personal self of man that, because he had chosen the way of the flesh, he must continue in that way all the days of his (earthly) life. He must live in sorrow and by the sweat of his brow, until he return to the dust out of which his body is made.

By these dicta therefore was mankind committed, by God, to

life on earth with, in each individual, the importance of the personal self paramount. Thus uncertainty, resentment and anger arose between individuals, with sebsequent remorse and bitter repentance. Thus was man committed to Hell. A life from which he must rise by his own efforts in gaining the enlightenment necessary to identify himself, eventually, with the spiritual entity which he really is, and to gain final ascendency over the physical body and senses.

And every woman who, deliberately and knowingly, tempts the animal nature or compulsive urge in man, sins, for this nature is a part of that which man must overcome before he can become immortal. Every woman who knowingly uses her sex to gain power over a man, sins, for she is serving the end of the little personal self in her, at the expense of the spiritual self, which can meet a man only in mutual love. For the coming together of the spiritual entities of a man and a woman really in love, in the orgasm of the sexual act, is more than a mere union of the flesh. It is a foretaste of the coming to oneness of the spirit, and there is some similarity between it and the merging with God experienced by the mystic (not in the immediate sensual effect). Sexual union experienced thus is holy.

Man and woman were intended, although separate entities, to work together towards the spiritual end. Woman as a help meet for man. In and through each other they can have a foretaste of the coming to oneness which has its climax on return to union with God.

With the final end clearly in view, the alternative paths seen, and the knowledge in them of the guidance of intuition which can keep them truly aligned, a man and a woman can act, when the conviction in them is strong and true, as a single entity. And they can reach enlightenment together. Not for nothing was Eve made from Adam's rib, and not from the dust of the ground. Not for nothing is she able to freeze him, and to make him sweat in turn. Hers is a great part in the salvation of mankind. At present it is, all too often, a hellish part. She must be shown true meaning and purpose. Then maybe she will respond truly. And then also will man respond truly to her. There should not be any resentment here due to misunderstanding. It may appear that the whole blame is being placed upon woman. That is not so. It should be understood rather that the initiative is with her, for a man is more dependent upon a woman for his direction than is often realized. It should be remembered too that a woman in this life will be a man in another life, and will then be on the opposite side of the equation.

Any woman who flaunts her sexuality before men, privately or in public, must be told that she sins, for she and all her kind together, add up to a terrifically potent incentive to the many men in whom sexual tension is increased by such actions. And sexual aberration and crime cannot but increase, while women flagrantly urge men on. This is not urging a return to Victorian days, but every man's wife and daughter is in increasing danger, while sexual aberration runs rife as it does today. And every man's son is suspect, for a man can stand only so much, and some are weaker than others. Despite their lack of restraint, those who give way are not wholly to blame. In many of these cases the blame must be shared by thousands of women who, by their actions have added fuel to the fire, until repression and frustration broke out into a hellish blaze. Some of the women responsible, particularly the younger ones, may not be conscious of what they do, but this does not make their conduct right. They must be told and made to realize that persistence means that they sin. Again this does not mean that we should return to old time prudery. There is a happy medium, which does not include flagrant display and deliberate attempts to stimulate the sexual passions of men. For this is what is being done today, and although, generally, we deplore the results, we do nothing whatever to prevent it.

Sexual intercourse is debased in having become, to many, a habit and even a pastime. This is a world-wide problem the solution of which is extremely difficult. A spiritual drive is necessary to balance the sex equation and this has been missing, for lack of inspiration, for too long.

Often if a man reacts to provocative actions or display by a woman, by attempting to force sexual intercourse on her or may-

116

be only to, what is colloquially called, 'make a pass at her', too many women will say that he is a filthy beast, or that he has a dirty mind. In making such remarks these women are often only showing their ignorance of the natural forces which impel a man to this compulsive urge. Forces which were in man as he emerged from the animals and were designed to preserve the species. Women must understand this and that they who, by provocative behaviour, hold men back to the jungle, are the very ones who were made to be help meets to men, to help them to climb from the animal level to a spiritual level commensurate with civilized development.

Woman has not yet realized in what she is intended to be a help meet to man. It is in his climb from the ape to the realization of himself as a spiritual being, made in the Image of God. To do this he must learn to control all the animal instincts which are in him, including this compulsive sexual urge. Until woman understands this and can help intelligently, man will be a very long time in gaining control, mainly because the sensual gratification is so attractive, and, with present day contraceptive convenience, now without the immediate consequences of childbirth. The deeper and long term consequences are hidden at present, and it is of these he must be made aware.

There is of course the danger that a man may use the foregoing argument to excuse a lack of self-discipline on his part. It is a vexed question which must be approached by each sex understanding better the feelings and the natural urges of the other, against a background on which they can see the designed reason, purpose and end of sex, man and woman.

The tendency today to arrange, through contraception, for man to give expression to this compulsive urge without restraint and without apparent consequences, is wrong, for it stops the necessity for the self-discipline, which is the most important lesson a man has to learn in life. It also means that his direction is reversed for, instead of an upward drive away from the Natural Phase, he is, in giving way to this sexual urge without restraint, acting like an animal. Not only this, but he is blinding himself in believing that consequences are averted because they are not apparent, and does not realize that there are consequences which will affect his destiny, distort his alignment, and so increase his suffering in the future. Promiscuity and subservience to the compulsive urge must be seen as a retrograde step. For we are at a point of climax, and something must be done about it if we are not to drift, willy-nilly, deeper and deeper.

Individually, man must rise above the body of flesh and fleshy satisfactions. This means that he must learn control over his senses and the habits formed by gratifying them. Sexual intercourse must be included for it is usually on a much lower scale than the ideal, and is undertaken as a rule primarily for sensual enjoyment. If however contraception is essential to control world population, which would allow man's sexual urge full scope, then his individual corrective is in periods of voluntary meditative retirement. This is essential if he cannot contain himself completely while living with a female. Even if he can, such periods are extremely valuable to any man.

Sexual intercourse should never be taken lightly. It should be the outcome of mutual love whether conception is intended or not. It should never be an occasion which arouses resentment in either partner. Man and woman must begin to understand each other's outlooks and motives better : what urges each to certain actions, and what in each causes anger and resentment. And when they understand these things better, then they must comply with the rule which Jesus gave, to consider their neighbours as themselves. Woman must understand that whether or not sexual intercourse can be placed and held on a high spiritual level is mainly up to her. She can and should have the initiative. If man is allowed to take and keep it, then an increasing lack of control and self-discipline is inevitable. By the constant sensual titillation which she maintains and allows to be maintained through various channels today, woman is playing into man's hands and is allowig the initiative to slip from her. Moreover she is gradually losing the respect of the very men she tries to please. She must quite firmly regain the initiative and must maintain her hold, if she is to help as was intended. She can ensure that the act is one which is kept for, or at least is only completely satisfactory in, periods of mutual love and understanding. Man never will do this on his own, for to him the act is too important in itself. It will not be easy for her, but there is so much to be gained that the effort is well worth while.

This subject has been treated at some length because it is so very important, not only for each individual and each couple, but for mankind as a whole. The tendency of present day civilization is towards making life easier for the individual. Easier, that is, in gaining the material things of life and for the gratification of the senses, it being thought that this is the way to happiness. Instead it is slowly being realized that with the constant speeding up of life which is necessary to satisfy the constantly increasing demands, mental tension is increasing tremendously and happiness becomes more and more elusive. Mental illness is increasing and probably much of the physical illness of today is due to the increase in mental tension. And so the temperature of Man's hell continues to rise, and will do so until he finds the way to relaxation and contentment in a simpler way of life, and with his little personal self subordinated to the welfare of his neighbours.

Simultaneously with this and partly consequent upon it, has come more and more relaxation of the all important self-discipline which holds men out of the jungle. And the very faculty of reason which first allowed man to break away from the animals, is being held to ransom by the discontented and undisciplined, whose number increases every year. So who can be surprised if it is said here that the trend of today's civilization, despite all superficial appearances, is towards the jungle. Not to the innocent jungle of the Natural Phase but to a jungle fouled by the evil of man.

Every boy born today is a new Adam, and every girl a new Eve, from the point of view of self-choice, and if they are to be saved from some of the hell of fear, uncertainty and frustration which is ours today and which is intensifying so quickly, they must be taught from the beginning to see things in proper perspective. They must learn that the personal self, with its lust for power and for sexual indulgence, must be controlled for the sake of the spiritual end of man. And all the learning, and all the book knowledge of the physical world, is of no worth to a man, who in his earlier years has not been given by his parents and other teachers, a correct spiritual alignment and a rigid training in self-discipline. Without these a man may rule the world, and yet be no more than a dead man.

The Bible:
Free-choice and Original Sin

It will have been realized by now, that man does not have free choice until the time comes when, realizing what and where he is, and in what condition he continues, and also that there is guidance available to lead him out if he so wishes, he then, and only then, is able to exercise that choice.

Christianity places man's free choice of direction in the Garden of Eden, where it believes him to have been a purely spiritual being until the choice was made. It therefore sets the blame directly on man from this point, because he chose the way of the little, personal, fleshy self, with its knowledge of good and evil, instead of continuing as a spiritual being. But with the new belief in 'The Fall' occurring, not in the Garden of Eden, but with the fall from The Mind Image to the actual creation, there was then no choice to make in the Garden of Eden, which in our new conception is the point at which the human emerged from the animal species. The development of thinking and the faculty of reason which caused man to emerge, are seen as a natural development of the evolutionary phase. It was not a suddenly bestowed gift from outside, with also a suddenly given choice of direction. A free choice of direction at this elementary stage of reason in man was impossible. As he broke gradually from the laws of instinct by means of his new found ability, he did not do so knowing any alternative. He had no choice then but to do so, and so committed no sin. He has not, therefore, continued to be born in the sin of his original ancestors ever since. With intuitional guidance so very weak, he could not possibly have followed it at that stage when instinct was still so strong in him. Consider how weak intuition is in the majority of men today after this long period of development from the beast, and it is obvious that it must have been so weak at first as not to be felt at all. And until it is felt strongly enough to give a man a sense of wrongdoing in ignoring it, it cannot be considered as a reasonable alternative. So, until the time came when man felt or knew this alternative, he did not have another route to follow, and self-choice for man only appears when, individually, he has in him some knowledge of the alternative way. That knowledge is in many men today, but still not in all.

There can be confusion here, and some may deny in man intuitive guidance, including the voice of conscience, but it is there surely enough. Certainly today it is mixed up, and some-times overlaid by man-made custom and taboo, which are drilled into the young until they become almost inherent. But as man develops, conscience can be distinguished by him, and becomes increasingly apparent with spiritual development. In fact uncom-fortably so, and it is in part the knowledge of it, and the conscious or semi-conscious attempted denial of it, which often constitutes one of the main psychic loads on a man. It is inherent, and he must come in line eventually. This is the second way, and free choice comes only with the conscious realization of it, not before.

Reincarnation

Will you try to clear your minds completely of all preconceived, deeply-rooted ideas, and consider reincarnation fairly and rationally? Reincarnation is the belief that man is essentially a spiritual being who has come from God, and has everlasting life. While on this earth, he is born in the flesh not once, but many times. He is here for the purpose of realizing himself as an essential spiritual being, and he returns again and again until that purpose is accomplished, after which he goes on in his originally conceived spiritual form, to his destined spiritual end. He is on earth, in other words, to find himself as he really is—not just a frame of flesh, blood and bone, but an enduring spiritual entity. Of how many that you have known can you truthfully say that in the single span of some seventy years they have certainly come to such understanding of themselves, and of God, and to certain belief in a life eternal hereafter? It must be agreed, that there are very many who do not reach this stage before they die. They have sinned in a greater or lesser degree during their seventy years here, as do we all. What then happens to them at death? Are all these sins automatically forgiven? Are the notoriously evil men we have all known, to be forgiven at death and admitted into a greater and happier life beyond, in the same way as very much better men than they? If not, what? Are they to be judged and, if found wicked by heavenly standards, consigned to some form of everlasting punishment without the chance of paying for their sins, and so redeeming themselves? Or are they made to suffer for their previous errors, and then given another chance to realize themselves? In view of the promise, that those who live by the sword shall die by the sword, is it not reasonable to suppose that this means that as we sin in the flesh, so will we suffer in the flesh? And that the promised punishment or torment, will be everlasting in the flesh until the purpose of man on earth is achieved? He realizes that at last he is the spiritual entity he was intended to become, then, having surrendered his little self, he merges with

123

God. Thus he finishes for ever with the body, and the everlasting punishment in the flesh comes to an end? This surely is what can be looked upon as justice and no-one who really believes in God, can believe in Him as being unjust. We must pay for what we take.

If we can agree with the foregoing, and surely most reasonable and intelligent people will, then there must be some way of ensuring that this law of recompense, this payment for errors, is carried out. Certainly it is not always done and a balance arrived at in one earthly existence. So then, reincarnation means that man, the spiritual enduring man, is re-born on earth, sometimes male and sometimes female, in different fleshy bodies. He goes through numerous lives on earth, with, between each, a long waiting period, during which he is enabled to look back over his previous existence and see the errors he has made. Then, at his next birth in the flesh, this backward look is erased from his consciousness, in all but exceptional cases, but the lessons learned from it help to guide him in his actions through his next incarnation. And so, through numerous lives here, he pays for his past mistakes, and slowly and gradually climbs from being unconscious of himself as a spiritual enduring entity. When he realizes this completely the law of recompense ceases, for at last he has produced a balance. He has paid for past errors and is acceptable for completely spiritual existence in the future. This realization can come at an earthly death, or during an earthly existence. It means that he has no more need for a mortal body which has served its purpose and is finished with. The contemplation periods between earthly death and re-birth are the times when man, looking back over his own errors of the past, passes judgment on himself in the realization of his errors. Their culmination is when, in the flesh, he is conscious of this realization and so identifies himself completely with the spiritual entity which is the real Man.

Most of you who read this believe, or at least wish to believe, in a personal God. Let us not attempt to make any strong appeal to the emotions, or they will take the place of reason. But emotion is in us, and its searchings also must be met. A real and true conviction of God can be only in a just, a merciful, and a loving God. To have a real faith in Him, we must be able to understand His ways sufficiently to see Him as just, without recourse to any drugging, re-iterated phrase, such as 'He knows best'. The intelligence and intellectuality of present day man demands more than that, and surely he is not asking too much. Even the prophets like Moses were given signs on which to base their faith. And if the signs which we are permitted to see, are only such as evil-doers escaping the results of the immeasurable evils of their lives here, or congenital cripples leading lives of frustration, anxiety, or even agony for no apparent reason, while others live in good health and with few cares, then faith is stretched to its limits if not beyond. Moreover, how can you account for the differences in environment and in temperament? How is it that some are born intelligent even to the point of genius, while others are dull and inept from beginning to end? Is all this reasonable or just, on the supposition of one span of life which is even more limited for those who are killed or die in their early years? Again, how explain that the sins of the fathers shall be visited upon the children, even to the third and fourth generation, unless the children are seen as the future lives of the same individual? And so they are. Each man is re-born in the flesh again and again, and each life follows on his previous lives, and so his past sins are visited upon him in the future. Surely this is reasonable, just, and understandable? Can we not then have faith with conviction in a just and a merciful God?

And, after all, whence comes the belief that we have only one existence here? I have read much of the Bible with an open mind not blocked by preconceived notions implanted there by others. I have read it patiently and painstakingly, and I cannot find in it any reasonable basis for such a belief. It seems to me that there is evidence to the contrary. We believe that there is life hereafter : that spiritual man has everlasting life. Everlasting life means life for ever, before and after the present, so why should we suppose that a spiritual man suddenly starts now, that he did not exist before as well as going on after? There is no good reason. In fact reason says the opposite.

Can you in fairness and with an urge to find out the Truth, dismiss reincarnation? Can you?

Take some evidence from the Bible. First look at Matthew xvi, verses 13 and 14, 'Whom do men say that I the Son of man am? And they said, Some say that thou art John the Baptist, some, Elias: And others, Jeremias, or one of the prophets.' Slightly different versions are also in Mark vi, verse 15, and Luke ix, verses 7 and 8. It is surely quite evident here that they accepted that the spirit of one who had died could be transferred to a body born later. And, mark you, it was not denied by Jesus.

There is also at least the implication, if nothing stronger, that Jesus accepted the general idea of reincarnation, that the spirit of one dead was inhabiting a body born later, for in Matthew xvii, verses 12 and 13, we have, 'But I say unto you that Elias is come already, and they knew him not, but have done unto him whatsoever they listed: likewise shall also the Son of man suffer of them. Then the disciples understood that he spake unto them of John the Baptist.' A similar statement is recorded in Mark, chapter ix, Surely this is very strong confirmation that Jesus saw in John the Baptist a reincarnation of Elias, and that such was the accepted belief of the times.

Then there is the prediction in Micah, chapter v, verse 2: 'But thou Bethlehem Ephratah, though thou be little among the thousands of Judah, yet out of thee shall he come forth unto me that is to be ruler in Israel: whose goings forth have been from of old, from everlasting'. What interpretation do you put on this? Surely the following is at least as good as any. Jesus had gone forth in the flesh time and time again, reincarnated again and again from of old, from everlasting.

Come now to the birth of Jesus. If Christians accept miracles, then they can accept this as a miracle with meaning. It pointed out that the essential spiritual Man, was not come of man but of God. Assuredly the fleshy body was not conceived of a virgin, that is, a virgo intacta, as was popularly and superstitiously supposed for so long. All know that the fleshy carcase of man comes of physical man and woman. But it is not realized that the enduring, ageless, spiritual entity is not a part of the physical body but is everlasting, going from physical life to physical life, building up all the way through experience and accumulated wisdom. And

God, at that time, could only point this in the superstitious understanding of men by, in this special case, seemingly severing the
conception from the usual channel. This was shown on the
paternal side as the virgin birth, and in later years Jesus himself
severed it on the maternal side in John, chapter ii, verses 3 and
4, 'And when they wanted wine, the mother of Jesus said unto
him, They have no wine.

'Jesus saith unto her, Woman, what have I to do with thee?
mine hour is not yet come.' When his hour came, then the fleshy
carcase might be returned to the woman who bore it, after the
essential spiritual entity which was the real undying Jesus had
left it. Until that time she had no claim on him.

After the birth of Jesus, the evidence thus given to men was
overlaid by the first, approximately, thirty years of his earthly
life. It was the life of a man among men. Then came the full and
blinding realization of his real stature—the flash of understanding of the Holy Ghost when he was baptized by John. 'And Jesus,
when he was baptized, went up straightway out of the water :
and, lo, the heavens were opened unto him, and he saw the Spirit
of God descending like a dove, and lighting upon him :' The
man thus realized his Sonship. He identified himself completely
in that moment with the higher, eternal, inner entity in him.

Then, the identification complete, came the work and preaching for God, he being in close intuitional contact the whole of the
time. And here lies the unseen crux which has been overlaid in
the minds of too many men by the image of the thorns on the
head and the nails in the body. From that time by Jordan, Jesus
was free from the law of recompense. He became as pure spirit,
though still weighted with the earthly body, still imprisoned in it.
And for him there could be no more punishment. But, consciously
and of his own free-will, he took upon himself the physical burden
of death on the cross for the sake of the Divine example. Do not
allow that bodily suffering, undertaken consciously and willingly,
to blind you to the greater agony of mind suffered during those
last two or three years. This was the unseen cross and a greater
and a more prolonged one than the final bodily anguish. Other
men since, have suffered as much bodily anguish for the sake of

their religion, but none like he the years of suffering in knowing that, though freed from sin and the payment for it, he would consciously take the burden of the physical cross, to enlighten those to come.

Is there anything in the whole of this which can offend an intelligent Christian? Surely not. This interpretation makes for a fuller, more vital and happier Christian religion than the world has yet known. It explains many things otherwise unexplainable. It throws light into dark places in the understanding and gives to man a clearer basis for the faith which he must have. It detracts not a whit from the glorious example, life and sacrifice of Jesus, while it gives to God that which should be His. It reveals greater glory than has been seen in full by men before, for they have only glimpsed it. Christianity is shown in full light and with a certain purpose, and with life ruled by a discernible justice.

In addition to all this note that belief in reincarnation was acceptable by the Christian Church until the sixth century A.D. It was held, amongst others, by great scholars of the church including Clement of Alexandria, Origen and Augustine. It was eventually rejected in 553 A.D. by the Council of Constantinople, but it would seem rather as a matter of expediency, because it did not fit in with other doctrines. For instance the dogma of special creation, that is the bringing into existence of man at a certain time, by Divine fiat, and not as an evolutionary being through natural development. Also the doctrine of original sin, that is, the belief that all men for all time are held responsible for the first sin on the part of the first man. It is obvious that something had to go. What a pity that it was reincarnation. It seems quite possible that, if the new interpretation of Genesis as given in this book had come in time, then the former acceptance of reincarnation might never have been abandoned. Remember that the doctrines concerned are the constructions put on the scriptures by men and are subject to error. It seems that the squint in the eye of Christianity (which Paul had helped to start), was set from the time of this final rejection of reincarnation in favour of the alternative doctrines.

No-one was to blame, and although we must look at the matter

128

with eyes and mind fully open, no-one should doubt the sincerity of those concerned, and no one should attempt to apportion blame. From its beginning Christianity has depended almost wholly upon the emotional appeal which carried it so far and wide, but also caused it so much trouble. For those responsible for the original creed and doctrine, were too close historically to the Cross and its emotional aftermath, and the squint in the eye is due to this intensely emotional appeal. And Christianity's very life, with its present doctrines, depends upon the maintenance of this emotional intensity which, as intellectual integrity becomes more and more important, will become less and less effective. Only corrective action, to eradicate this over-emotional tendency, will remove the initial errors.

In our new belief, we see that it is unnecessary to accept the sudden creation of man at a certain point in history. We see him now as a risen ape rather than a fallen angel, for he rose of and from the animals in the general evolutionary cycle, and we see that the symbolic breath of God which transformed him, was the arrival at the stage of reasoning. This breath of God which made him a living soul, was the faculty of reason which was necessary if he was ever to know and return to God. And The Fall had nothing to do with the Garden of Eden. The first man committed no sin which needs to be passed along the line. He merely acted as God intended he should in taking the fleshy, physical road, until eventually he exercised his self-choice in leaving it, and becoming, as originally in The Image, purely spiritual as he returns to God. The Fall, as we now see, was the descent from the original Mind Image of God, to the commencement of creation in the physical sphere.

Since doctrines can be changed, it is not too late to remove the squint from the eye. Not too late to accept a further injection of the 'breath of life', that is if humility sufficient to the occasion can be achieved. Not too late to lift the ceiling from the psychic Heaven, to reveal the spiritual Absolute.

Heaven

Christianity as a religion is on a psychic rather than a spiritual level, and so sees in Heaven, which is mainly a psychic state, the final goal of man. Heaven is the intermediate state, in which the soul finds itself on release from the physical body.

Here, as has been said before, comes a scanning of the whole memory film of the past life in the flesh and, with intuitive guidance strong, due to the loss of the physical body and the overpowering physical sense impressions, all the errors of the past are seen, and a new alignment of direction is made, ready for the next life in the flesh. So the events which have passed, make the destiny for the future. These are the intermediate destinies, which can be controlled partly by man himself in the flesh, when he knows of them.

This is where the soul comes more strongly into contact with God, through intuitional guidance without the physical body and senses to damp it down. It must be seen as a wise move on the part of The Creator, for without such easements from the overpowering Natural Phase through the physical body, the spiritual entity could not stand against it, and eventually overcome it. So the wearing out of physical bodies allows for periodical easement and at the same time for reorientation as stated previously.

When considering the matter of intermediate destinies, and that the conduct of a man in one physical life influences what he experiences in his next life, it should not be taken to the extreme that if a man murders another in his present life, he will be murdered in turn in his next life. The balance as drawn is not necessarily in kind. It works, not in such detail as that, but on the level of planes of consciousness. There is a very long ladder of planes of consciousness up which a man climbs, from the beast to God, and the intermediate alignments as made in the resting periods in heaven, are on the rungs of the ladder. In other words the plane of consciousness for the start of his next physical life, is determined in this resting period. As has been said before, this

130

is not the sole arbiter of the next life's experience, but it is the main, and spiritual arbiter. The plane of consciousness thus arrived at, combined with the heredity of the physical life into which the realigned spiritual entity is born, plus the general environmental conditions, set the direction for the coming life on earth.

In heaven we experience life eternal, that is life out of time. Time is of no importance, and the events of many years can appear before one in a few minutes. And the probable several hundreds of years duration of a resting period, can no doubt pass very quickly. It may be that the period can seem to vary, according to our condition and to what we need to assimilate.

The enlightened, free from the law of recompense and intermediate destiny, do not again need this psychic heaven and, on passing from their last physical bodies (the last death), merge with God.

Compulsion without Conviction

Individualistic gods of divine origin are out-dated today, and religious belief must move with the times or die. This does not mean necessarily that basic beliefs need be altered, but only their presentation. If the presentation cannot be altered to suit the times, then there is something wrong with it, and it should be revised or, if necessary, scrapped and replaced. If the basic beliefs of a religion are such as will not permit of an altered presentation, then there is something wrong with them. For basic Truth must be applicable to all people at all times. It was before man was, and not it, but man, must change. And if a religion does not fit all people at all times past, present and future, then the religion is wrong, and must change or die. It is not necessarily wholly wrong, so that partial change or realignment may be sufficient. But stubborn adherence to the out-dated beliefs which came of past environmental conditions, and equal only to the intellectual understanding of their day, will certainly bring decline in the greatest religion.

Compulsory dogma is the shackle forged by the arrogant. Free choice as given by God to man, gives the lie to all such compulsion. Man is intended to be a free individual entity, and it is to the individual that free choice is given, not to the few, not to the chosen, but to each member of mankind. Each one has his free choice of continuing to suffer, or of being delivered from suffering. God exerts no compulsion on a man. He provides the means of guidance which a man takes when he will, but not when dragooned into it by compulsory dicta. Compulsion without conviction is the only right description of any such method, because if there is conviction there is no need of compulsion, and compulsion it is if the possibility of salvation is denied, excepting through a church, membership of which entails compulsory belief in a man made creed.

Dogma as a measure of self-defence in the early days of a religion is one thing, and tolerable if considered temporary for its purpose. But continuance of it with compulsion, after a religion is established, must lead in time to slow strangulation. In short, suicide.

Doctrine, which like God's regulations is always within limits, is necessary, but only as guidance, and must never become so rigid that it is intolerant of change. The limits of its tolerance must be used as required, so that the Natural, the Psychic and the Spiritual Phases work together in one huge and closely knit cycle throughout all time. The cycle from everlasting to everlasting.

The Holy Ghost and the Holy Spirit

There is a great confusion here, for the Biblical references are thoroughly mixed, and surely few of the writers made real distinction between the two terms.

In the view of this new belief and for the purpose of this book, when the terms are used The Holy Ghost is taken to be the inner spiritual entity which is in every man and is a unit of The Creator. It is the ghostly entity which begins a separate development as man, but is unseen and mainly unknown, until eventually it is consciously recognized at the day of an individual's enlightenment and identification of himself with that in him, and when he becomes at one with it as the Son of God. This is the day of the baptism of the Holy Spirit, or intuitional guidance, which has been shown symbolically as an external visitation from above, but which is in fact an internal identification. And realization of the actuality cancels the need for symbolism which is necessary for the unaware, such as the symbolism in the case of Jesus.

The Holy Ghost said in Solomon: 'The Lord possessed me in the beginning of his way, before his works of old. I was set up from everlasting, from the beginning, or ever the earth was. When there were no depths I was brought forth: when there were no fountains abounding with water. Before the mountains were settled, before the hills was I brought forth: While as yet he had not made the earth, nor the fields, nor the highest part of the dust of the world. When he prepared the heavens, I was there: when he set a compass upon the face of the depth. When he established the clouds above: when he strengthened the fountains of the deep: When he gave to the sea his decree, that the waters should not pass his commandment: when he appointed the foundations of the earth: ...'

Spiritual man, the Son of God, was made in The Image, before physical creation began. And it is the inherent knowledge which

134

is in physical man which draws him, guides him, shows him his objective, to which he must rise again once more in the complete likeness of The Image, purely spiritual and free of the flesh. He must make the ghost real.

And Jesus was, and is, not the only Son of God. He was like to us in all respects excepting that he was an outstanding example. Symbolically he said, 'This is my body', and he broke the bread. And this, the breaking of the fleshy bodily hold, we were, and are, to do in remembrance of what he did. There is no need to break bread and consume it in remembrance of him, excepting it be purely symbolically, and with the symbolism fully realized. We are to break the bodily hold, the sensuous hold, in remembrance of him, and because it is the only way a man can come to God. And in the shedding of his blood he likened himself to the sacrifice of animals by the Children of Israel, in ratification of the covenant.

We are not to remember the body and the blood as symbolic of what his enemies did to him, but as symbolic of what he did to himself, that he broke and sacrificed his physical self for the sake of his spiritual self. And that is what we are to do. That is the example we are to follow.

And if you consume bread and wine as symbolic of the broken body of Jesus, remember that they must, at the same time, be symbolic of your own physical body which the spiritual you must break and consume, before you can find the same end as Jesus, as Son of God.

For the Sons of God, as men, were made in The Image before ever a physical body was created. And as God became man in that original image, so man must become God in the end. And the Kingdom of God comes gradually as each individual realizes his Sonship.

To be filled with the Holy Ghost, means suddenly to receive enlightenment and to come to the certain conviction or recognition of oneself as the inner spiritual entity—the ghostly entity now fully recognized.

We should seek, above all things, intuitive guidance, one of the promptings of which is known as the voice of conscience. For surely this is that which Christians call The Holy Spirit, although seemingly they do not always distinguish between it and The Holy Ghost. For the purpose of this book then, The Holy Spirit will be taken as The Holy Guidance or Intuitive Guidance.

Virgin Birth

The child born of a woman is a complex being. Its fleshy frame comes of the sexual union of the human father and mother, but not the spiritual entity which is born therein. In that frame is reincarnated a spiritual being which dwells there for the earthly life-time of that frame only. It is there by Divine law, and the habitation is chosen as being suitable to the particular development of that spiritual being. In this respect therefore every birth is a virgin birth, for the real being, the spiritual being inside the fleshy humanly conceived frame, is not derived from the mother and the man.

The revelation which was given to mankind in respect of Jesus, that his was a virgin birth, has been regarded by Christians as something unique to this one man. Seen however with a belief in reincarnation, it is something which applies to the birth of every human being. Revelation of it through Jesus, the spiritual Jesus, was an example to other men. Seen in this way the revelation of the virgin birth of Jesus, may be taken to confirm reincarnation.

The tradition is found also in other religions and applies, for instance, to Gautama the Buddha.

The so-called miraculous or supernatural becomes natural in later years as the intellectual growth of man enables him to have greater understanding. So-called miracles are happenings which are not understood on the intellectual level of man at a particular point in history. Thus, with the beliefs expressed in this book, a little more of the supernatural becomes natural and another miracle becomes, not ordinary, still wondrous, but at least understandable. Once more we can rationalize that which was superstitious.

Slowly, as we proceed by means of the intellect from ignorance to intuition, understanding of more and more superstitious beliefs must open up and the joys of fitting the miraculous into the known be increasingly savoured. Superstition will decrease slowly but surely, for superstition is ignorance and nothing can prevent the growth of understanding of all things.

E*

A Few
Short Thoughts
and Aphorisms

A Few Short Thoughts and Aphorisms

In unknowing comes absolute surety beyond the knowing.

Mis-applied mysticism is magic, and in magic the right end may be lost.

The secret harm you do to one, can easily outweigh the manifest good you do to many.

The unaware continually ask God for help. The enlightened come to one with God and help themselves.

The enlightened have no morals, but morals are necessary to enlightenment.

If I stand still the clouds move. If the clouds stand still I move. If we both move there is confusion. If we both stand still there is peace.

Curiosity dies as wisdom dawns.

Still value the physical body, for it is only through the death which is life, that freedom can be found from the life which is death.

If we are to know man we must know God; and if we are to know God we must know man, for these two are indivisible, and, knowing these two we must then know nature, for these three are indivisible.

There are few things which are more important to the spiritual progress of a man than a real sense of humour. For if a man laughs at himself, it means that he takes himself seriously.

Man can only understand that which he is, and there is nothing he is not.

Humility in the face of God need not entail servility in the face of man.

We only know what we experience.

Life is the key to death and death is the door to life.

Nothing, literally nothing, in life is free. You can have almost anything you care to wish and work for, but every jot and tittle must be paid for.

Imagination does not cease with the death of the physical body.

Loss of memory is an improper term. It should be, correctly, loss of the ability to use memory, for memory cannot be lost, and will survive death of the physical body for as long as the soul requires it.

The physical human body is at once the greatest help and the greatest hindrance to finding God.

The most difficult thing you will ever have to do is to forgive yourself.

While there is one man left to speak, there will be at least one other left to misunderstand him.

Physical life is to be cherished, for only through it can we find the way out of it.

No-one is born in sin but everyone is born in error—deliberately conceived error which has to be corrected by us.

When we die we do not go anywhere in the spatial sense. We are still here—where else would we be?

Some living in physical bodies today were also in physical bodies when Jesus was in his last one.

Apparent humility can be learned : real humility is earned.

To reach enlightenment does not mean that suddenly one knows everything, but means that suddenly one experiences complete identification, and reaches a level of consciousness on which everything is knowable.

Conclusion

The altar has been smeared with blood too long;
Now let the bloody dust consume its blood,
And do not in your superstition make
Necessity of evil; seek the good
That lies beyond the broken flesh and bone
Without the price that more may have to pay,
If you in ignorance and fear do shun
A kinder and a more enlightened way.
For animal and man have paid a price
Too high for what already is achieved,
And you do but refuse the offerings
If all in Truth is not to be believed.
There is a restlessness that stirs in Heaven,
And sighs which earthly ears have not yet heard,
And sorrow that man's hell sinks deeper yet
Because he has refused to hear the Word.

Conclusion

I've come round full circle for I started with Christianity, left it to be an Agnostic, then became an Atheist for a short time, and then, though always an Agnostic, returned by a mixture of Spiritualism, Mysticism and intellectual probing, together with a gradual alignment of ethical conduct through self-discipline and some degree of self-denial, to the cleansing personal revelation, which allowed of the focus on the underlying thin gold line of general revelation. This led me to undertake a short investigation of the great religions of the world. Only then did it become apparent that what I have called The Focus, that is, the general revelation, was really a combination of parts of most, if not all, the surviving great religions plus a number of additional features. It was then I think natural that I should first bring Christianity into focus, fitting the necessary parts of other religions into it, rather than the other way round. Its shortcomings for me had been what started me on my search for something better, I had access to its literature, and was able more easily to observe it in operation, and to see the results on individuals as well as on the general public. Moreover I feel that I owe Christianity a double debt of gratitude, first for giving me a grounding in decent ethical behaviour, and second for presenting to me a theology which shocked and antagonized me, when I reached the necessary intellectual maturity to become aware of it, and apply reason to it.

Looking back, it seems that I can sum up my work (that is apart from the bread and butter aspect essential to bodily survival), as a lifetime spent in the attempted rationalization of superstition. (The definition of rationalize here is: to render conformable to reason.) I have used what, for me at least, has been a near-scientific process, that is I have proceeded only as far at a time as I had sufficient proof to satisfy my always extremely sceptical mind. I admit that I cannot provide documented proof of any of it, for never more than about two people besides myself knew anything about all this, and only one of

147

them, my wife, was constant throughout, but I did, at various times, tell her my findings before any proof was even set in hand, so that she could be an independent check. Some theories were formed as I proceeded but were ruthlessly thrown out if disproved, and no attempt was made to 'wangle' around them. After all it was myself I had to convince, not anyone else. Various small experiments were undertaken which are not mentioned, as for instance when I spent a considerable time experimenting with a theory of dreams, and a time process.

When I say I did not proceed further without sufficient proof for myself, I mean that anything accepted by me before I proceeded further, had to be based on my own experience. I know very well that this will not be sufficient proof for many other people, because their proof must be based on their own experience, for a man knows only what he has experienced. I suggest therefore that any reasonably intelligent man can produce the necessary condition in himself if he is ripe enough. He must have so developed that he is prepared to spend many years in the process and to sacrifice much of the sensual satisfaction of life by living in a moderately self-disciplined way. (I do not mean to the extreme of asceticism.) It may, however, take only a fraction of this time. One of the main reasons for wishing to publish this is, therefore, that to a man in an advanced stage of preparedness, it could give the necessary alignment and impetus to carry him into the right condition in a very short time. He will then be able to provide his own proof, whereas otherwise it might take many years, or he might not achieve it at all in this particular lifetime.

Having digressed somewhat, we must return to the consideration of Christianity. I can never be other than pleased that I left it, and I can never return to it as it is taught today. To me it is full of superstition, over-emotional, and without any possibility of giving intellectual satisfaction. And yet there is so much of the evidence which I believe to be correct, on which it bases its beliefs, that it cannot be set aside. The evidence includes, as has been seen, a considerable portion of the holy book of Christianity, the Bible, and in particular those parts concerned with the creation and general evolution of this world and of mankind, and of the life and example of its main prophet in Jesus of Nazareth.

A new integrated belief must surely come to be. All others are only partial. Some may weep at the foot of the cross. Some tread the everlasting treadmill. Some may find the peace of the Void. Some may suffer and burn. Some may go through death and return. And it all adds up to ONE. The diffused must mingle to give the essence. Their pride will be hurt, they will kick against the pricks, but, starting slowly, the belief will show dimly for a while, before it grows into a bright light. It is all a slow process of man's emancipation from superstition, and superstition still has the great majority of mankind in its grip, although most of them as yet do not realize it. It is indeed unlikely that this civilization will see the end of superstitition, for mankind has run so far off the rails, and bogged down so deeply, that it is doubtful if anything can put it back on the rails again. Probably all that can be done is to give the next civilization the best possible start. In the meantime individuals can, if they wish, help themselves.

Do not think that this suggests the end of the world. It is however, a statement that physical man can stand only a limited degree of hell and that, when he reaches that degree he must burn up and start again in a cooler atmosphere, and with better alignment. And the only way he can do that collectively, is through the ending of one civilization and the starting of another.

This ending and restarting seems to be on the way. Although no doubt regarded as a shocking calamity by the majority, it is not so really, for in the long run it is a good and a wise happening. The next civilization will not start as far back as did the present one, but at a point from which the original errors of this one will be covered. After that it will be on its own, but inherent in it will be the lessons of this civilization. It might be possible by rightly guided concerted action by all mankind, to avoid such a, what some would call, calamity. The possibility of such understanding and cooperation is extremely doubtful, however, even if the necessity for it were realized in time. Material development has run much too far ahead of spiritual development, and worse, runs headlong downhill at an ever increasing pace, while those who see themselves as spiritual caretakers of mankind, sit over-comfortably on their spiritual backsides.

Men like Copernicus and Darwin showed how wrong had been some of the previously accepted interpretations of revelation. One would have thought that religious bodies would have heeded such warnings, and themselves have promoted a spiritual campaign with the object of re-checking, and if possible widening and expanding generally, all the revelations having bearing on their religious outlooks. But the years, and indeed the centuries pass, without any significant enlightenment coming from them, so that it appears as if they are either completely satisfied with what they already have, deny the possibility of further light ever being thrown on their beliefs, or have not the spiritual quality neces-sary to find greater light. Most branches of science in the mean-time forge ahead, and reveal more and more facts which may, and no doubt will, eventually have bearing on religious belief. And the general scientific range is opening wider and wider. Understanding of the Natural Phase is mainly, and of the Psychic Phase partly, the work of general science, but what is being done in theology, either in looking for the new or in revising the old? Is it working to meet and keep abreast of the others, or is it waiting to be swamped by them? Is it lagging behind, and is this the reason why religion is losing its grip? Because it is over-content with the early elementary stages of the search, and will not sanction the necessity for continued progress in keeping with general intellectual progress? If so it is surely time that it awakened to the necessity; for man and humanity, individually and collectively, are in a parlous state, and above all are in great need of spiritual assistance.

Many times in the last few years I have felt a great thankful-ness that I seem to be able to tear down some of the veils which screen the face of Truth. Sometimes when very weary or when nerves were a-twitch, I would think back to the peace and bliss of the mystic union that I experienced years ago. To rest peace-fully in that state without care or consequence, was something which could not be left without, occasionally, a backward glance. I have never been sorry that I did leave it, for it was a purely personal, intermediate end, which lacked ultimate reason and purpose. So it had to be left, and will not be re-captured completely until earthly death. For once left, the further work undertaken is a hard taskmaster, and will not ever let go while time lasts.

The veils come down easily or with difficulty, some in a few weeks, others in as many years. It needs ceaseless, non-forced persistence. The first thought in the mind distorts the veil, the second thought whisks one away out of reach. If there is still some distortion in reception, it has to be ferreted out. It has however become easier to see when this occurs, and to remove it. The veils are never-ending while time lasts, and will be as long as men last. But each one removed lightens the darkness a little.

Occasionally I try to fight my way back to the state of thinking and believing which used to be mine, but I cannot do it. I have become used to working mainly intuitively, and to do otherwise now I find so fatiguing that I soon stop. It amazes me now that I was ever in such a state for so many years. And yet I know that the majority of mankind see life from the opposite angle, that is, from the one I have left behind. And because of that many will not be able to accept much of the truth set out in this book. It will be to a large extent unreal, for they still look outwardly instead of inwardly.

Although Christianity has been made the main object of focus, and the partial truths of other religions have been used to throw light on the framework of the partial truths of Christianity, this does not detract from the truths of these others. If I had been born and bred of an eastern race, then no doubt the opposite would have occurred, and perhaps Hinduism would have been the object of focus, while parts of Christianity, amongst other religions, would have been fitted in. To Jews, Moslems, Hindus and Buddhists, I acknowledge a debt of gratitude for the parts of their religions which have provided light for me, even though the taking of such light was not of my own volition. By this I mean that the continuous thread which is now mine, came to me first but vaguely understood, and I had then to search throughout world religion generally, to find where the parts of it belonged.

It was only then that it became obvious, that this new understanding was made up of parts of each of the world's great living religions and philosophic beliefs, together with some new material. There was nothing deliberate or mechanical about the process on my part. The integration came before the realization of it.

To Christianity I owe a debt for giving me a preliminary training sufficient to my early years, before reason was once more well established in me. In this book I am trying, amongst other things, to repay the debt by, so I believe, shedding further light on Christian evidence which, if accepted, can mean a greater understanding. How many will be able to accept it I do not know. Many will not, I think, because they do not wish to, being too comfortable to wish for disturbance. Many no doubt will react thoughtlessly with abuse. None of this will be my concern. I have done what I had to do. Not lightly, for there has been, in the last nine years, an intensive period of often wearying work, in addition to all the fumblings and probings of the previous thirty years.

I believe that, in addition, this book may help some to believe in God, who otherwise might not. This is, in itself, sufficient justification for seeking publication. I know now, having recently searched the great religions of the world for just one which would satisfy me, that there is not one which can. There is not one which has more than partial truth but, the partial truths of each, together with some newly revealed truth in this revelation and reasonably intelligent, if not very detailed understanding of evolution, have given what is to me a fairly complete and satisfying picture.

Christianty, if you will allow your emotions to rule you, will give the fervour to promote faith even against reason, but today it needs to be combined with the cold reasoning of philosophy, in order to satisfy the increased intellectual standard of men.

Those Christians who know anything of the religion and philosophy of the East, usually deplore, what they call, the coldly philosophical outlook on meaning and purpose, rather than on sin, forgiveness and love. They seem to forget that one outside the Christian religion may see Christians at the opposite extreme, wallowing in feelings of guilt, and limiting their understanding by over-accenting the emotional. Human emotions have to be catered for, but they have also to be held firmly in check.

Christian tendency, to me, seems to be an apology for its conception of God. In other words, although Christianity insists that man is the original sinner, and to blame for all the sin and evil and suffering of the world, it knows deep down that God, having made man and being basically responsible for all his actions, is basically responsible also for all the sin and evil and suffering. Hence their obsession with making Jesus the Christ the only Son of God, so that the punishment shall return through him, creating an apparent state of justice, in that the punishment is thus lifted from us, even though at the same time insisting that it should rightly be ours. This is necessary to Christians, because they cannot see all men as being, eventually, Sons of God, and each therefore rightly bearing his own part of the consequences. So they want the best of both worlds, that of man and that of God, without allowing either to take the punishment due, and they transfer it to the one lone figure on the cross, and then talk of love, justice and mercy. To me it seemed, long ago, and still does today, that although others than Christians crucified Jesus in the flesh, Christians continue to crucify him day by day. If in so speaking I offend any sincere true believers, I regret it. If they have sincere belief, then nothing that I or anyone else can say will destroy it. If their belief is so shaky that what I say makes them uncertain or uncomfortable, then it is time they overhauled their belief, to make sure that it is not a ready made one, too easily accepted and not carrying real conviction.

It may be that the strong feeling of guilt running through Christianity is due to this, that they are attempting, whether consciously or not, to pass the blame from themselves to Jesus, and their over-emotional attitude towards this lone figure, and worship of it, come of this, so that Jesus has for many, I feel, become what was never intended, as a shutter drawn across the face of God.

If God is responsible for the whole of creation, he is so for all that happens throughout creation and its evolution to its end. Therefore if there is to be no duality in the original creator, then

God is responsible for the results of all creation, men included. For it was God who made man in His Image, in His Likeness, and it was God who gave man free choice, and by the last action he must accept, despite any warnings he gave, responsibility for wrong action : for if he had not intended there should be wrong action, there was no point whatsoever in giving free choice to man. God made man for God's own ends, not for the ends of man.

Christians therefore are over-sin-conscious because, due to neglect of intellectual understanding, they apportion blame wrongly and insist (even while attempting to pass it on), that men must suffer for the responsibility of God, even though, to them, men are other than God. No wonder then that they carry a load of guilt with them always. It is not until you have got rid of it, that you realize it was there.

Let it be quite clear that there is no attack here upon Jesus, or upon what he did, for I believe that he put himself on the cross, that is, acted in such a way, regardless of consequences, and in love of God and mankind, that there could be no alternative. Thus he made of himself an unsurpassed example of the breaking of the body or the fleshy hold, so that the spirit might be freed and able to return to the wholly spiritual original. The evidence of his own words, if these are correctly reported, points to the deliberation of this. It is therefore the Christian interpretation of it which is in question. Not the historic event, and certainly not the quality of his sacrifice, or his supreme love of God and of mankind shewn in it.

It is not suggested here that salvation cannot come through the idea of Christ. Taking Jesus as a symbolic example a man can, when his time comes, and he cannot do it before, make his own sacrifice of all that the fleshy body means, for the sake of return to the spirit. He cannot do that however, until he has balanced his own scale through suffering, right thinking, and right action. The sacrifice of the example had to be the sacrifice of one become sinless. And the sacrifice of every individual of all that the physical world and the physical body mean, must be by one who has made himself sinless. All offerings before this are mere words and gestures.

154

Jesus never could have been fully man by being only tempted. Even if he did not sin in his last life in the flesh he had lived many lives before. To be fully man he had to take the same deliberately planned wrong road as was intended by God, to succumb to the temptations, and to rise out from them freed from their shackles. Then with the conviction of experience in him, he was ready for the symbolic path of the example which lay before him. And the experience at Jordan was the enlightenment which has come to others also, the sudden flash of realization and identification of oneself with the inner entity (which suffuses the whole body as lightly as a dove alighting). That this happened at a confessional baptism does not make such procedure necessary. The baptism, or washing away of sin, was symbolic only, and many reach enlightenment and find God, who have never been baptized.

Baptism by John the Baptist was the outward and visible sign of repentance, to which was given a remission of sins. To be baptized was an admission that one had sinned, and had repented. Christianity insists that Jesus was without sin, but this is because Christianity wishes to see him that way, and is not based on any good evidence. To say that it is on the evidence of his conduct during his ministry is not enough, for all men who really receive enlightenment and pass through the judgment day, are unable to sin again. They may err, though rarely for they are in close touch with intuitive guidance, but they will not persist in error, and therefore do not sin and are free from further individual consequences.

In Jesus at Jordan the true inner repentance and the true enlightenment, coincided with the outer visible sign of baptism. He, in that moment, really balanced his scales and, in the illumination which followed, seized upon the intuitive guidance which assured that he would not again sin. Leaving out the scant details of his life up to twelve years old, the only picture of him as recorded, is as sinless for the period of his ministry, which is variously believed to have been between eighteen and thirty-six months. It is on the evidence of this picture only, that Christianity insists that Jesus was sinless throughout his life. For the previous eighteen years approximately (twelve years old to thirty years old), there is no evidence whatsoever, and this period is the most vital in the life of a man with regard to his sinning or not sinning. Whatever a man be, in these formative years he is the most subject to temptation, and at the same time the most venturesome in trying all that presents itself to him, and persisting in what appeals, even despite warnings. It is strange that no record was made of his earlier life. If it was, then it must have been either suppressed or destroyed. Without it, Christianity has not a good case in saying that Jesus was always without sin.

It is difficult to see any good reason why he should have allowed himself to be baptized, if it were not that he did, indeed, wish to make public confession of sin and of repentance, for in those days he was not known as he was later, and to have done it only as a gesture, would have been of little value. That day for him surely, was the culmination of a very long journey from everlasting, through many earthly lives. On that day he was born of the spirit. Only after that, when he was purged, could he enter into his real work of receiving his revelation, and in taking up his work as a glorious example.

To me, this gives a much greater meaning to Jesus than is accorded by Christianity, for while still being as great an example, he has risen from Son of Man to Son of God, through the very sin which man commits, along the very path which man takes. To me he is a greater figure as one who was tempted, sinned, and of his own volition through intuitive guidance, rose out of it to sinlessness, than as a man who never succumbed to temptation.

I am nearly finished. In my early years, Christianity threw out a challenge to me which I had to take up. My acceptance of it was quite unconscious and it is only in retrospect over the last few years, that it has become apparent. Nevertheless it has been so, and it has taken most of a lifetime to justify the feelings of disgust and anger, which were mine when I turned my back on the religion of my youth. And, having regard for the impetuousness of youth, and the terrific depths of feeling which are plumbed by the young, I think maybe they have been justified. Nine years ago when I was receiving my revelation, I remember one phrase which came through very clearly. It was, 'Christianity has a squint in its eye.' And so I maintain it has. If in this book I make an attack on Christianity, it is sincere, and of experience, and I do not come to the fight with empty hands. If I attempt to alter something, I try to offer as much back in replacement. In fact, I hope, more.

Jesus founded his church on the rock of the faith evidenced in Peter, and it was sufficient to the understanding of the day. If he had attempted to give a real intellectual understanding to the superstitious and intellectually undeveloped minds of the day, they would not have responded. Today, understanding must be built on the twin rocks of faith and reason, to suit the less superstitious and more intellectually developed minds of the present. Nothing stands still, not even understanding God. Particularly not understanding God.

There is a sadness in me when I think of the depth of the rut mankind is in, and the steepness of the hill down which it runs. Then, looking at the Church of the West, I see how it loses nothing of the old and creaking misconception and misunderstanding, and binds nothing of new, deeper and stronger understanding. 'And I will give unto thee the keys of the kingdom of heaven: and whatsoever thou shalt bind on earth shall be bound in heaven: and whatsoever thou shalt loose on earth shall be loosed in heaven.'

What but the understanding of God's processes for mankind, can be intended here? 'Seek, and ye shall find.' 'Knock, and it shall be opened unto you.' And the greater understanding you shall bind, or capture, on earth shall be bound in heaven. In other words, the understanding found here shall be of use in heaven, in your alignment for the future. And the misconceptions and misunderstandings loosed on earth, shall be loosed in heaven, also assisting in the new alignment for the next life on earth.

'Feed my lambs.' 'Feed my sheep.' On what? Feelings of guilt? Strict and binding laws for all alike without reference to development? You shall do this, or you must do that, the same for all? Why did Jesus say sheep, and then, separately, lambs? Because he knew that the development and understanding of man varied in individuals, from just above the beast, to just below God. And man, therefore, had to be fed an individual understanding, equal in each to his capacity for it. That is the real food for the lambs and the sheep. That is the real healing for the sick, for the healing of the mind is even more important than the healing of the body. And today man cries out for a greater understanding, and he cannot find it. His mind is rent by, on the one hand the wish to believe in God and in the message of Jesus, and on the other by the continuous evidential revelation of material scientific discovery. And only the greater understanding which can be found on earth, can be used in heaven to heal the rent. And only the loosing of old superstition can permit of the new understanding.

How different mankind might have been today, if the keys of heaven had only been used to open up to the understanding of man the role of heaven in the process of enlightenment, for heaven is the place of judgment or alignment, and the launching place for us all on new trials, and new chances in further life in the flesh, with the eventual certain glory of a sinless transition to the living God. And they were given the chance but they were blind, and the blind have led the blind, and maybe will continue to do so. Is it too late? Is the age of miracles indeed past? If so I must stay alone in my new and, for me, certain faith of The New Interpretation.

At least let it be said of my criticisms that I have not been merely destructive. I have been constructive, and in this respect I would like finally to say, that the future depends mainly upon the layman, and in addition to a complete overhaul of interpretation and doctrine, I believe that other changes are necessary too. Emotional religion is necessary in the preliminary stages, but reorganization is required so that training shall grade upwards, particularly for laymen, through the mystical to the philosophical, so that eventually there may be an integration which will bring the true and irrevocable enlightenment to a man.

Many times in my younger years, in common with many others of course, I have wished that I might have been one of those in bygone days, who were able to make voyages of discovery, and find new lands and strange things not known before. And even up to comparatively recent years, to read of the old pioneers made me ache, almost physically, for the feel of a felling axe in my hands, or the smell of a sweating horse in my nostrils, and for virgin land under my feet.

Gradually the hopes, and then the dreams faded, and I was left more and more isolated in the midst of a civilization which I liked less and less.

And then, fairly recently and quite suddenly, an unthought of vista opened up, and man became boy again, and eagerly and happily, at last set out on a voyage of discovery beyond all dreams. And today I am content, for the voyage is for the duration, and will leave me well over the horizon. For this time, as I believe, I shall not return, and only the living Infinite will lie ahead.

Meditation

Sometimes in the morning as the light of day is breaking,
Sit you down and ponder over thought of what you really are,
What you were and what you will be, and establish a relation
'Twixt yourself and other men and God, and yon fast fading star :
In the quiet of the dawning which no man has yet polluted
With the artificiality which he makes his today,
Still the thoughts which dart so restless, never sleeping, never
    ceasing,
And become so still inside you that surroundings pass away :
And in you find such quietude, a listening internal,
Such a prayerful alertness for a message you may find
To come stealing almost timidly, 'tis intuition speaking
To you in the deep recesses of your still, unhampered mind :
'Tis a moment which, once captured, cannot ever be forgotten,
'Tis a moment that is holy, when the God in man shall speak
To the mortal in submission to the greater force within him,
And where quietness is strength and where a noise but shows the
    weak :
For 'tis not with words or actions that a man shall tell his story
When he meets the one eternal in the quiet of the mind,
But with humble acquiescence to the will which waits in silence
For the quietness to reach the minds and hearts of all mankind :
And as slowly you return to notice that the sun has risen,
And that peace has now been shattered with unholy man made
    noise,
You may sigh to find the veil once more descended over spirit,
But you'll face the trials of the day with calmness and with poise :
For a minute with the Maker gives assurance to the spirit
That it is of stuff eternal which will never pass away,
And the cloak which doth envelop it and soon shall die and
    perish,
Will release it to the brightness of an everlasting day.